ANDREW LEVINS

NEW
HOLLAND

ACKNOWLEDGEMENTS.

FOR BIANCA

Thanks for always doing the washing up

Thanks to my family—Mum, Dad, Em and Tepi. My grandparents, uncles, aunties and cousins.

My staff at The Dip (RIP) and everyone who came to eat there.

Jimmy Sing, Hana Shimada and everyone at Goodgod Small Club.

Mitch Orr, Dan Hong, Thomas Lim, Louis Tikaram, Morgan McGlone and all the other actual chefs who don't hate me.

My amazingly supportive friends, everybody at Heaps Decent and everyone who came along to one of my barbecues over the years.

John and Dell Khalil, Mel Leong and FBi Radio.

Thomas Walk and Graeme Gillies for the photography, and Jodi Wuestewald for styling.

Lliane, Bronwyn, Stephanie and everyone at New Holland.

FOREWORD

Levins has been a good friend of mine since we started Heaps Decent (an initiative dedicated to nurturing and developing underprivilged and emerging young musicians and artists) together many years ago. He has always been an adamant music fan, a superb DJ and, I would find out later, a dedicated cook.

Travelling together on many tours I would notice that Levins blended influences from all over the world in everything he does. He is a creator first and foremost – many times during our tours Levins has hosted parties where he has put me to sleep with multiple burgers cooked up in his tiny kitchen.

Fast forward to 2011 and Levins opened his own restaurant, The Dip, where he has heightened the art of hot dog nachos and mojitos named after dancehall superstars, as well as putting his original spin onto other contemporary dishes. He may be eclectic but isn't that the point? Who wants your typical burger and fries in a cardboard box anyway?

Wesley Pentz, aka DJ Diplo

CONTENTS.

INTRODUCTION.

I'm Levins. This is my book. I wrote it in between kitchen shifts, DJ sets and eating.

I've been DJing and cooking food for almost a decade. My main focus was DJing up until two years ago, when my girlfriend Bianca and I decided to open a restaurant together inside a bar and nightclub that a friend of ours ran, which we've recently closed. Before that we used to host huge parties in our backyard for about 100 of our friends. The music would be loud, the drinks would be plentiful and, most importantly, the barbecues would be blazing day and night, cooking up course after course of fun and fresh food. They were some pretty legendary parties.

When we opened our restaurant we wanted to make sure we kept that party vibe from the barbecues. The food had to be fun, a nice mix of guilty pleasures made with fresh ingredients. You could bring a massive group of friends, buy a few jugs and get your hands covered in cheese while sharing nachos, or come through late at night to have a quiet hot dog by yourself. We drew inspiration from our favourite junk food and fast food chains, the staples you find on the menu at a diner in the middle of nowhere, and cooked them our way, adding new ingredients and different cooking methods without changing the original nature of the dishes too much. You can't screw around too much with the classics.

This book combines the recipes of the dishes we loved to cook every night at our restaurant with the food we used to serve at our backyard parties years ago. They're tried and true hits, perfect for entertaining big groups or for when you want to turn your kitchen into that diner in the middle of nowhere.

Eat up.

TEN THINGS TO GET STARTED

1. AT LEAST ONE OTHER PERSON

Never cook alone. Cooking alone is two things: crappy and boring. You should have someone to cook for. Friends love food, tell someone you'll cook for them and they will be your friend. Problem solved. Even better though is someone to cook with, cherish them and add bacon to all their meals. Especially their desserts.

2. A BARBECUE

If you can't fit 20 friends inside your kitchen you'll be doomed forever to be alone in there, should you ever invite them over for an eating party. Get yourself an awesome barbecue and you'll achieve that awkward neck-only tan you've always wanted in no time, plus an infinite amount of mates can stand around you, in awe of your grilling skills. Food just tastes better when it has been cooked on a barbecue, and most of the recipes in this book are perfect barbecue fare.

3. A WEBER

The Weber barbecue is the next step up from your standard gas grill barbecue. A sleek black metal ball on legs, the Weber Kettle barbecue will kick all your meals in the balls, then smoke them until they're tenderer than anything you've ever eaten before. A Weber allows you to prepare food the best way ever – by smoking it for hours at a low heat, ensuring unbelievable tastiness. They are a little expensive but worth every penny, and the more you use your Weber the better you get at unleashing its smoky magic.

4. A DEEP FRYER

Did I just say the best way to prepare food was by smoking it? I may have overlooked the equal best way to prepare food – deep frying it! Sure there are healthier ways to eat chicken wings, hot dogs and even cupcakes, but once in a while you just need that deep crunchiness that your deep fryer can provide. You can deep fry in a frying pan, but you'll avoid many potential burns and accidents if you invest in a proper deep fryer.

5. PLASTIC SQUEEZY SAUCE BOTTLES

A fun name for such an important tool. Plastic squeezy sauce bottles are essential for showing off all the amazing sauces you're going to make from this book – just pour in the sauce, dressing, mustard or mayo and you'll be squirting out beautiful squiggles over hot dogs like a Renaissance artist. Draw your partner's name in chipotle mayonnaise with a hot chocolate fudge love heart around it and they'll be squeezing you before you can say 'mustard and mayo zig zag'.

6. A FOOD PROCESSOR
Chopping up vegetables for salsa by hand is a drag, man. Buy a food processor and save hours of potential eating time, and even the smallest food processor or blender will make it easier for you to blend sauces, mix ice cream batter and make salsas like a champion. Buy one today!

7. AN ICE CREAM MAKER
Ice cream is the best dessert ever, so naturally half the desserts in this book feature it. You're gonna need to churn that ice cream or else it'll get all icy and weird. You can get a simple ice cream maker for $20, if you have a little more money to spend you can get one with a built in compressor. It's like controlling the weather, except its ice cream!

8. A MANDOLINE
How else do you get those radishes paper thin? A mandoline is a screechy little violin thing, add an 'e' to the end of it though and you've got a sweet little contraption that slices your vegies nice and thin and adds an element of danger to all your food prep – I've almost lost most of my fingers to my mandoline. Get one so you can experience this exciting fear in your kitchen!

9. A BAMBOO STEAMER
You probably already have one to bring frozen dumplings back to life when you're hungover. Bamboo steamers are perfect for steaming bread, and steamed bread is the secret to a good hot dog.

10. A SILICONE BASTING BRUSH
When you start slow cooking massive pieces of meat you're gonna want to slather them with gallons of sauce – and the best thing to do it with is a silicone basting brush. The bigger it is the better!

FRIED
STUFF

Start this recipe 6 hours before you want to eat it | Serves 6

Assuming you've spent hours pickling cucumbers, then waited weeks for them to become tasty dill pickles, the most logical thing to do now is crack open a jar and deep fry them! 'Frickles' are deep fried dill pickle chips. They're the perfect mix of crunch and vinegary goodness. Dip them in some ranch and you have the ultimate beer snack.

8 large dill pickles (store bought or see
   Sauces, Salsas, Salads & Sides)
2 cups buttermilk
2 cups flour
1 teaspoon salt
1 teaspoon paprika
1 teaspoon garlic powder
1 cup Ranch Dressing (see Sauces,
   Salsas, Salads & Sides)

Using a mandoline, slice the pickles 4mm (1/8 in). Fill a bowl with the buttermilk and submerge the pickles in the buttermilk. Leave them fully submerged for 10 minutes.

   In another bowl place the flour, salt and spices and mix well to combine.

   Take each pickle round from the buttermilk and dip it into the flour, making sure it's completely coated. Place battered pickles in a container lined with baking paper, making sure they're not touching each other. Stack layers of baking paper and pickles into the container until all the pickles are used. Seal the container and freeze the battered pickles for at least 4 hours.

   Heat cooking oil in a deep fryer or frying pan to 180°C/350°F and fry the pickles for 4 minutes. If your deep fryer is small you may need to fry in batches. Once fried, place the frickles on paper towels to soak excess oil. Serve with Ranch for dipping.

FRICKLES

Start this recipe 1 hour before you want to eat it | Serves 6

The classic Buffalo wings recipe, found everywhere in the United States – this one is adapted from the back of the Frank's Hot Sauce bottle, which is about as classic as you can get. You won't find a better hot sauce to make hot wings with. It's pretty easy to find on one of the many websites that import American food products.

2kg (4lb) chicken wings
1 cup Frank's Hot Sauce (or substitute
    with Tabasco sauce or your fave hot
    sauce)
2 tablespoons butter
1 cup Ranch Dressing (see Sauces,
    Salsas, Salads & Sides)

Cut the wings at their joints into 3 segments. Discard the tips.

Heat cooking oil in a deep fryer or frying pan to 140°C/280°F and fry the wings for 12 minutes, until the skin starts to brown. Remove from the oil and drain on paper towels. You can freeze the wings after this point if you want and fry them up to serve later.

Heat the deep fryer up to 180°C/350°F and fry the wings for 5 minutes until super crispy.

In a pan on the stove, melt the butter over low heat. Add the hot sauce.

Place the wings into a large plastic container and pour the hot sauce over the top. Place the lid on the container and shake until the wings are coated in hot sauce.

Serve immediately with some Ranch for dipping.

HOT WINGS

Start this recipe 1 hour before you want to eat it | Serves 4

Fried chicken is so important. Scientists have proved that everyone should eat a whole fried chicken to themselves at least once a year. Fried chicken is best kept simple. The Colonel may have his 11 secret herbs and spices, but this recipe barely needs any to still be incredible.

1 whole chicken, cut into 8 pieces, skin on (ask the butcher to do this, or use a sharp knife and do it yourself, it's not hard)
600ml (20fl oz) buttermilk
3 cups plain flour
2 teaspoons salt

1 teaspoon freshly ground black pepper
¼ teaspoon cayenne pepper
1 tablespoon finely chopped coriander (cilantro)
1 cup Chipotle Mayo (see Sauces, Salsas, Salads & Sides)

Place chicken pieces in a bowl and pour over the buttermilk. Place chicken and milk in the fridge for 30 minutes.

In a large plastic container, combine the flour, salt and peppers. Add the pieces of chicken and place the lid on the container. Shake the container for about a minute, until the chicken is completely coated in the flour. Heat cooking oil in a deep fryer or frying pan to 140°C/280°F and add the chicken. Cook for 15–20 minutes, until the batter coating the chicken is deep yellow in colour. Remove the chicken from the oil and set aside.

Increase the deep fryer or frying pan heat to 180°C/350°F. Fry chicken for 2–3 minutes, until golden brown. The batter should be nice and crispy.

Transfer the chicken to paper towels to soak up the excess oil. Sprinkle chicken with the coriander and a little salt to taste. Serve with Chipotle Mayo.

FRIED CHICKEN

Start this recipe 6 hours before you want to eat it | Serves many!

Hand cut fries are hell to make but totally worth it. If you start making them in the morning you'll be chowing down on perfectly crunchy fries by dinner. The recipe says 2kg (4lb)of potatoes but feel free to make it 4kg (8lb) or 10kg (20lb)! If you're going to make the effort in the first place you may as well make a truck load of fries for all of your friends. Nail it and you'll probably make some new friends too.

2kg (4lb) Russet potatoes, skins on salt water

Start by washing your potatoes and cutting them into chips about 1½cm (½ins) thick. Wash the fries thoroughly in cool water.

Fill your biggest pan with water and 2 tablespoons of salt. Bring it to a rolling boil on high heat and add the chips. Let them cook for 10 minutes.

Remove the fries from the boiling water, drain and refrigerate for at least 2 hours.

Heat cooking oil in a deep fryer or frying pan to 160°C/320°F and fry the chips in batches for 6 minutes, until they start to turn yellow. Do not overcrowd the fry baskets. Remove them from the oil and allow to drain. Refrigerate for another 2 hours. You can freeze them at this point and fry them later if you want.

Heat the deep fryer to 180°C/350°F. Fry the chips for another 6 minutes, until golden and crunchy. Dust with salt and serve with ketchup – we serve fries with Chipotle Mayo or topped with salsa (see Sauces, Salsas, Salads & Sides) and cheese, and I thoroughly recommend you do the same!

HAND CUT FRIES

Start this recipe 1 minute before you want to eat it | Serves 1

Shaker Fries used to be my favourite thing on the menu at fast food joints when I was a kid. You'd empty your fries into a bag, rip open the flavour sachet, dump it over your fries and shake the bag, coating them in bright orange powder. It was the very definition of a flavour explosion. Here's my take on it.

One paper bag
1 big handful of hand cut chips, freshly fried and piping hot
1 teaspoon Chipotle Salt (see Sauces, Salsas, Salads & Sides)

Open the bag up wide and place the chips inside. Pour the Chipotle Salt over the top of the fries and fold the top of the bag over tightly. Shake the bag like a Polaroid picture for 30 seconds.

Eat the fries directly out of the bag. Don't be a snob about it, use your tongue to lick your fingers clean.

SHAKER FRIES

Pluto Pups have many different names depending on where in the world you eat them. Corn Dogs, Dagwood Dogs – I always knew them as Pluto Pups, a big deep fried hot dog on a stick, that would beg to be eaten whenever I saw one at a fair. My parents never let me eat them but guess who's in his twenties, owns a deep fryer and can do whatever he wants now?

8 kosher beef frankfurts (you can use other kinds but kosher are the best. You'll find them in delis, and the kosher section of the supermarket)
8 wooden chopsticks
1 cup cornmeal (you can also use polenta ground up in a mortar and pestle)

1 cup plain flour
¼ cup sugar
4 teaspoons baking powder
1 cup milk
1 egg, beaten
1 cup ketchup or tomato sauce
American mustard, for serving

Pat the frankfurts dry with paper towel. Carefully insert a chopstick lengthwise into each frankfurt, leaving 5cm (2ins) of chopstick sticking out one end and set aside.

Mix all the dry ingredients together in a large bowl. Add the milk and egg and stir until the batter is smooth.

Heat cooking oil in a deep fryer or frying pan to 180°C/350°F. Hold each frankfurt by the end of the chopstick and dunk it in the batter. Ensure the whole dog is coated in a thick layer of batter. Put on a pair of thick rubber gloves for safety and, holding the chopstick, place each frankfurt into the hot oil so that the whole thing is submerged in oil. Slowly roll it between your fingers for about a minute, then release and leave it to fry for another two minutes until golden. Once cooked, transfer the dog to paper towels to soak up any excess oil.Dip the tip of each Pluto Pup into the ketchup and squirt a zig zag of mustard down one side to serve. These are also awesome with Chipotle Mayo (see Sauces, Salsas, Salads & Sides).

PLUTO PUPS

Start this recipe 1 hour before you want to eat it | Serves 4

Hush Puppies supposedly earned their name during the American Civil War, when soldiers would throw bits of fried corn bread at their barking dogs to 'hush the puppies'. Decades after the war these fried little balls of awesome would inspire a brand of shoes that my mum used to wear. Cool story, huh?
If you've got a little leftover batter after making Corn Dogs or Pluto Pups, you should use it to make a bowl of Hush Puppies! They're really easy and taste great.

1 cup cornmeal (you can also use polenta ground in a mortar and pestle)
1 cup plain flour
¼ cup sugar
4 teaspoons baking powder
1 egg, beaten

¾ cup milk
1 teaspoon hot sauce or Tabasco
¼ cup spring onions (eschallots), finely chopped
OPTIONAL: 1 cup Pulled Pork (see Slow Cooked Stuff)

Mix dry ingredients together in a bowl. Add the egg, milk and hot sauce and stir until smooth. Stir in the spring onions. If you are adding Pulled Pork stir it through with the onions.

Heat cooking oil in a deep fryer or frying pan to 180°C/350°F. Drop a spoonful of batter into the hot oil. It will rise to the top after 10 seconds; allow it to cook for a minute until the batter is browned and crispy. Remove from oil and drain on paper towels.

Serve on the side – or serve with some Ranch (see Sauces, Salsas, Salads & Sides) as a starter.

HUSH PUPPIES

Start this recipe 40 minutes before you want to eat it | Serves 4

I'm really sorry there aren't more tacos in this book, but these are so good that maybe it's the only taco recipe you need! Track down some decent corn tortillas for this recipe. You can use other white flesh fish, but I think snapper is best as there's less bones and it fries really well.

1½ cups self raising flour
1 teaspoon smoked paprika
1 teaspoon chipotle powder
salt and pepper to taste
1 egg, beaten
1 x 375ml (12½ fl oz) bottle of beer, pale ale, draught or pilsner
4 snapper fillets, or other white fleshed fillets, halved lengthwise

8 corn tortillas
1 cup Radish & Cucumber Salsa (see Sauces, Salsas, Salads & Sides)
1 cup Red Cabbage Slaw (see Sauces, Salsas, Salads & Sides)
1 cup Jalapeño Cream (see Sauces, Salsas, Salads & Sides)
lime wedges to serve

In a bowl, combine the flour, paprika, chipotle powder and a sprinkle of salt and pepper. Whisk in the egg and gradually add the beer, whisking until batter is smooth. Heat cooking oil in a deep fryer or frying pan to 180°C/350°F. Dip fish fillets into the batter and fry them, two at a time, for 4 minutes, until batter is golden brown and crispy. Transfer the fillets to paper towel to absorb the excess oil. Serve the fried fish in a corn tortilla. Spoon about a tablespoon each of salsa and slaw over the fish. Serve tacos with Jalapeño Cream and lime wedges.

FRIED FISH TACOS

SLOW-
COOKED
STUFF

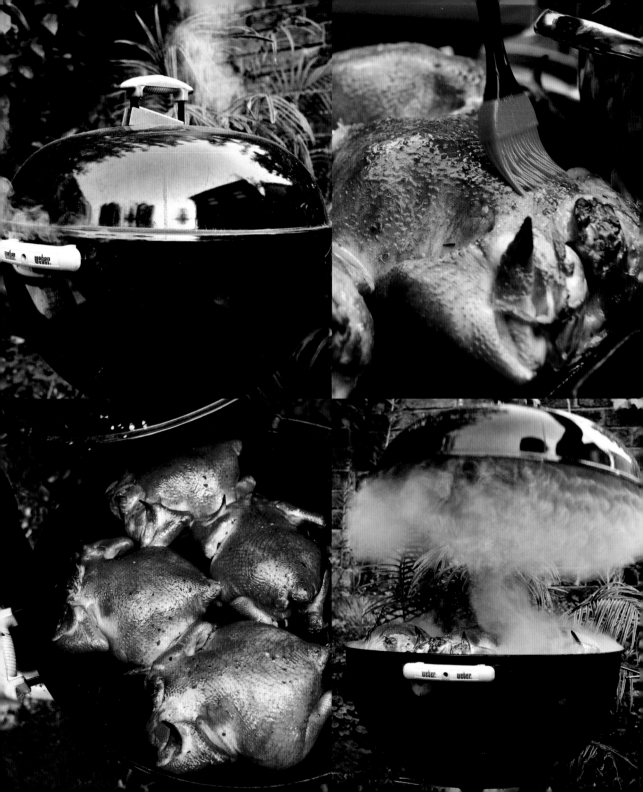

THE SLOW COOKING
MUST-DO'S

1. BE PATIENT! It's called slow cooking for a reason: it takes ages! The longer and slower you cook it for the better it's gonna taste so make sure you have enough time to give your meats the slow justice they deserve.

2. SMOKE IT UP. There's no better flavor than smoky meat. Buy some woodchips, soak them and add them to the hot charcoal beads about once an hour. nothing beats the combo of charcoal and smoke. The ultimate barbecue taste!

3. BASTE YOUR MEAT. Make sure you have plenty of sauce on hand to slather onto the meat each hour of cooking.

4. KEEP A METAL PAN OF WATER NEXT TO THE CHARCOAL BEADS. This will help keep the meat from drying out.

5. REST THE MEAT ONCE ITS DONE. I know you've already waited hours for it to cook but you're going to have to wait half an hour more. Wrap the meat in foil once it's cooked and let it sit so the juices can redistribute through the meat.

Start this recipe 1 day before you want to eat it. | Serves 2

These juicy ribs will have you asking yourself one important question: do I like lamb ribs more than pork ribs? It's a tough call, although lamb ribs definitely have more underground cred. 'Pork ribs are so mainstream, man.' I was eating lamb ribs before anyone even heard of them

2 tablespoons olive oil
4 cloves of garlic, minced
2 sprigs fresh rosemary, finely chopped
2 teaspoons salt
2 teaspoons freshly cracked black pepper

1kg (2lbs) lamb ribs, cut into 4 rib segments
2 cups woodchips, soaked in water (applewood is best for smoking lamb, or cherrywood if you can get it)

Combine the oil, garlic, rosemary, salt and pepper in a bowl. Spread mixture evenly over lamb ribs so that the whole surface is coated. Wrap lamb in cling film and let sit for an hour in the fridge.

Assemble some heat beads on only one side of your Weber. Light the coals and get the heat to 110°C/230°F. Place a water filled drip tray next to the coals and place the cooking rack on top. Place the lamb ribs on the cooking rack away from the direct heat of the coals. Drop a handful of woodchips over the coals and place the lid on the Weber. Cook the ribs for 4 hours, making sure the temperature stays at 110°C/230°F. Remove lid and add a handful of woodchips to the hot coals every hour or so, replacing lid after each addition. After 4 hours, move each rack of ribs over the coals and cook for 2 minutes a side, uncovered. This will burn most of the fat from the ribs. Remove the ribs from the Weber and wrap in foil, allow to sit for 15 minutes before eating the hell out of them!

LAMB RIBS

SMOKED PORK RIBS

Tearing apart the bones with your sauce-covered fingers to get every last bit of delicious smoky meat – ribs have got to be the most fun food to eat. These are the kind of ribs you'd request as your last meal before you get taken to the electric chair. I sincerely hope everyone reading this avoids such a fate.

4 racks of pork ribs
2 cups cola
¼ cup cider vinegar
2 cups woodchips, soaked in water
  (applewood or hickory are best for
  smoking pork)
2 cups Barbecue Sauce (see Sauces,
  Salsas, Salads & Sides)

For the rub:
½ cup brown sugar
2 tablespoons garlic powder
2 tablespoons salt
2 tablespoons cumin
2 tablespoons sweet paprika
2 teaspoons cayenne pepper

Mix the rub ingredients together. Apply rub to the ribs so that they are completely coated in the mixture. Wrap the ribs in cling film and refrigerate for 2–12 hours. The longer you leave them, the better they are.

Unwrap the ribs and place them in a plastic container. Pour the cola and vinegar over the top of the ribs and seal the container. Refrigerate for 12 hours.

Assemble some heat beads on only one side of your Weber. Light the coals and get the heat to 110°C/230°F. Place a water filled drip tray next to the coals and set up the cooking rack. Place the ribs on the cooking rack away from the direct heat of the coals. Drop a handful of woodchips over the coals and place the lid on the Weber.

Cook the ribs for 4 hours, maintaining a heat of 110°C/230°F. Remove the lid and add a new handful of woodchips to the coals every hour or so.

After 4 hours, remove the lid from the Weber and using a silicone basting brush or pastry brush, apply a thick coat of the Barbecue Sauce to the ribs. Flip the ribs over and apply the Barbecue Sauce to the other side. Repeat this flippin' and bastin' process every 15 minutes for the next hour.

Remove the ribs from the Weber and wrap in foil. Allow them to sit for 20 minutes before tucking in.

Start this recipe 3 days before you want to eat it | Serves many

1 x 6-8kg (12-16lbs) bone-in pork shoulder, skin removed
2 cups Spicy Barbecue Sauce (see Sauces, Salsas, Salads & Sides)
3 cups woodchips for smoking, soaked in water (the best woodchips for pork are applewood or hickory)

For the brine:
1 cup brown sugar
½ cup salt
2 dried bay leaves
1 cinnamon quill

For the rub:
1 cup salt
2 cups brown sugar
1 cup smoked paprika
1 tablespoon cayenne pepper
2 tablespoons garlic powder

PULLED PORK

DAY 1: In a saucepan over medium heat, warm 2 cups of water. Add the brown sugar and salt and stir until dissolved. Add the bay leaves and cinnamon quill to the water and simmer for five minutes.

In a plastic container or plastic bag large enough to hold the pork shoulder, add 4 cups of cold water and a cup of ice. Add the dissolved brine mixture to the cold water and submerge the pork shoulder in it. Cover the shoulder with more water so it is completely submerged. Transfer the container to a fridge and let the pork sit in the brine for at least 12 hours, but no more than 16.

DAY 2: Remove the pork from the brining solution and pat dry with paper towels. Combine the ingredients for the dry rub and apply the rub all over the pork shoulder, making sure to cover the entire surface. Wrap the shoulder in cling film and let it sit in the fridge for at least another 12 hours, up to 24.

DAY 3: Take the shoulder out of the fridge and set it aside to reach room temperature while you light the barbecue.

It's smoking time! You need to heat your Weber up to 110°C/230°F, and keep it at this temperature for a good 10 hours. My favourite way to do this is the 'snake method'. Line a row of heat beads two thirds along the wall of the Weber. Line another row of beads in front of the other and ensure all the heat beads are close to each other and touching. Take the woodchips out and scatter them over the heat beads.

What you have just created is one painfully slow fuse that, once lit at one end, will slowly light each heat bead over the course of 8 hours, ensuring no more than 4 cubes are lit at once and keeping the temperature nice and low. You will still need to monitor the barbecue to make sure the temperature stays where it should.

Use fire starters to light one end of the heat bead 'snake'. Fill a drip tray with water and place it in the middle of the Weber. Once the first beads have lit and turned red hot, place the top rack over the beads and place the lid on the Weber to warm it up. Make sure the opening on the rack is directly over the coals so you can adjust them, and add woodchips if you need to during cooking.

Place the pork shoulder on the top rack with the fat side facing up. Make sure it's above the part of the Weber where there's no woodchips, away from direct heat. Put the lid on the barbecue and leave it to cook for 2 hours, checking the temperature every 20 minutes or so to make sure the 'snake fuse' is working its magic.

After 2 hours, lift the lid on the smoker and baste the pork shoulder all over with the Spicy Barbecue Sauce, using a silicone basting brush or a pastry brush. Repeat this every hour until you use up all the sauce. This sugary sauce will give the shoulder a nice crunchy outer layer, once it's done.

Leave the shoulder to smoke for 8–10 hours. Ensure the temperature stays at 110°C/230°F by adjusting the Weber's vents – closing them will reduce the heat, opening them will increase the heat. Use an internal thermometer to check that the shoulder is between 80-90°C (176-194°F). Remove the pork from the Weber and wrap it in foil. Let it rest for 30 minutes to an hour.

Remove the shoulder from the foil. Find the bone in the shoulder – it should slide out from the meat easily. Using your hands or two forks, pull the meat into small chunks. Separate the fat from the meat and place the meat in a bowl. Eat the Pulled Pork directly from the bowl by itself, or use it to make: Pulled Pork Nachos, Southern Smoke, Pulled Pork Banh Mi (pictured, opposite), Pulled Pork Hush Puppies – the possibilities are endless.

SMOKED TURKEY LEGS

Start this recipe 1 day before you want to eat it | Serves 6

If you've been to Disneyland you've probably seen someone walking around holding an enormous turkey leg, looking like Fred Flintstone. If you were smart enough to eat one yourself you would've discovered they are almost better than the rides! For the complete effect wear Mickey Mouse ears while you're eating them. Have a friend dress up as Aladdin and try and get his autograph.

½ cup brown sugar
1 cup salt
6 large turkey legs, skin on
½ cup spicy Barbecue Sauce (see Sauces, Salsas, Salads & Sides)
2 tablespoon coriander (cilantro), finely chopped
2 cups woodchips (hickory works best when smoking turkey)

For the rub:
1 tablespoon onion powder
1 tablespoon garlic powder
1 tablespoon paprika
2 teaspoons sage
2 teaspoons freshly cracked black pepper
2 teaspoons cumin
4 tablespoons olive oil

In a pan, combine the brown sugar and salt with 2 cups of water. Over medium heat, stir until the sugar and salt have dissolved. Pour dissolved brining solution into a plastic container; add 6 cups of ice-cold water and stir. Add the turkey legs to the container and add more cold water to make sure the legs are submerged. Refrigerate legs for 12 hours. Remove the turkey from the brining solution and pat dry with paper towels. In a bowl, combine the onion powder, garlic powder, paprika, sage, pepper, cumin and olive oil and mix well.

Rub the mixture over the turkey legs so the whole surface of the skin is covered, and set aside. Assemble some heat beads on only one side of your Weber. Light the coals and get the heat to 110°C/230°F. Place a water filled drip tray next to the coals and set up the cooking rack. Place turkey legs on the cooking rack away from the direct heat of the coals. Drop a handful of woodchips over the coals and place the lid on the Weber.

Cook the legs for 4 hours, maintaining a heat of 110°C/230°F. Remove lid and add a new handful of woodchips to the coals every hour or so, replacing lid after each addition.

After 4 hours, remove the lid from the Weber and using a silicone basting brush or pastry brush, evenly coat the turkey legs with Spicy Barbecue Sauce. Replace lid and cook for half an hour more. Remove from Weber and allow to stand for five minutes.

If you like, sprinkle the legs with coriander and serve.

Start this recipe 1 day before you want to eat it | Serves 4

This is a sweet and straightforward way to smoke chicken. The end result is awesome – the chicken skin turns a terrific dark orange and the smoky flavour gives the chicken a taste almost like ham.

½ cup brown sugar
½ cup salt
1 whole chicken, skin on
100g (3½ oz) salted butter
1 cup spicy Barbecue Sauce (see
    Sauces, Salsas, Salads & Sides)

In a pan, combine the brown sugar and salt with 2 cups of water. Stir over medium heat until the sugar and salt have dissolved. Pour dissolved brining solution into a plastic container big enough to fit the chicken; add 6 cups of ice-cold water and stir.

Place the chicken in the plastic container and add enough water to fully submerge it. Refrigerate for 12 hours.

Remove chicken from brining solution and pat dry with paper towels. Melt the butter in a pan over a low heat and stir in the spicy Barbecue Sauce. Use a silicone basting brush or pastry brush to evenly coat the entire chicken in the buttery Barbecue Sauce. Keep leftover sauce in the pan, you'll need it again later.

Assemble some heat beads on only one side of your Weber. Light the coals and heat Weber to 110°C/230°F. Place a drip tray filled with water next to the coals and set up the cooking rack. Place the chicken, breast facing down, on the cooking rack, away from the direct heat of the coals. Drop a handful of woodchips over the coals and place the lid on the Weber.

Cook the chicken for 2 hours, maintaining a heat of 110°C/230°F. Remove lid and add a new handful of woodchips to the coals every half hour or so, replacing lid after each addition.

After 2 hours, remove the lid and baste the chicken with the remaining Barbecue Sauce. Turn it over and baste the other side. Replace lid and cook chicken for another 2 hours with the breast facing up, basting one last time an hour before you finish cooking.

The chicken is done when it reaches between 80 and 90°C (176-194°F) internally, or when the juices run clear. Remove it from the Weber and allow it to sit for 15 minutes before carving and serving.

SMOKED CHICKEN

DYNAMITE BEEF CHILI

This slightly sweet and totally spicy beef chili is in its element spooned over hot dogs, fries, corn chips and pasta.

1 tablespoon olive oil
1 white onion, finely chopped
1kg (2lbs) beef mince
¼ cup plain flour
1 teaspoon cayenne pepper
1 teaspoon chipotle powder
1 teaspoon chili flakes
1 teaspoon garlic powder
1 teaspoon smoked paprika

1 teaspoon cumin
2 teaspoons salt
375ml (12½ fl oz) beer
1/3 cup cider vinegar
1/3 cup ketchup or tomato sauce
2 tablespoons treacle
2 tablespoons Worcestershire sauce

In a large pan, warm the oil over medium heat. Add the onion and cook for 5 minutes until it starts to brown. Add the beef mince to the pan, stirring quickly with a wooden spoon to break up lumps, until the meat is browned.

Combine the flour, cayenne pepper, chipotle powder, chili flakes, garlic powder, paprika, cumin and salt in a bowl and add to the pan, stirring to mix into the mince.

Add the beer, vinegar, ketchup, treacle, Worcestershire sauce and two cups of water. Stir well and bring the pan to the boil. Reduce the heat to low and simmer for 2 hours or until all the liquid has reduced. Season with salt and serve over fries, with pasta or as a Dynamite Chili Dawg (see Burgers, Sandwiches & Hot Dogs).

Start this recipe 4 hours before you want to eat it | Serves 6

Beyond enticing. One of the world's greatest foods braised in two of the world's greatest drinks – it has to be good!

2kg beef short ribs
375ml (12½ fl oz) bottle of beer
2 cups cola
1 cup vinegar
2 cups ketchup or tomato sauce
2 tablespoons treacle
4 chipotles in adobo

For the rub:
2 tablespoons garlic powder
2 tablespoons smoked paprika
2 tablespoons onion powder
1 tablespoon cumin
1 tablespoon salt
1 teaspoon cayenne pepper
1 teaspoon white pepper

Mix the rub ingredients together in a bowl. Apply the rub to the beef short ribs, coating the surface evenly.

Sear the short ribs on a grill or barbecue until browned all over. Set aside.

In a large pan, combine the beer, cola, vinegar, ketchup, treacle and chipotles. Set the pan over medium heat and stir well. Add the short ribs and bring to the boil. Decrease the heat to low, cover, and simmer for 3 hours, stirring every half hour to prevent mixture sticking to the bottom of the pan.

After 3 hours, remove the ribs from the pan and take out the bones. Shred the meat with two forks and set aside.

Leave the sauce in the pan simmering, uncovered, until thickened. Skim the fat off the top. Add a few spoonfuls of sauce to the shredded meat and stir it through.

Serve as a sandwich (see Burgers, Sandwiches & Hot Dogs) nachos (see Slow Cooked Stuff) or make up something cooler and serve it as that.

BEEF SHORT RIBS

Start this recipe 4 hours before you want to eat it | Serves 8

Serve these spicy black beans as a side dish, or as a topping for nachos.

4 cups dried black beans
1 tablespoon olive oil
1 white onion, finely chopped
2 garlic cloves, finely chopped
4 chipotles in adobo, finely chopped
¼ cup coriander (cilantro), finely
   chopped
1 tablespoon salt
2 tablespoons lime juice

Clean and rinse beans. Place beans in a large pot, then pour over enough water to reach 5cm (2ins) above the beans. Cover, and soak overnight. Alternatively, bring the pot to the boil and cook for 15 minutes, cover, reduce heat and simmer for an hour. Drain beans and set them aside.

In another large pot, warm the oil over medium heat. Add the onion and cook for five minutes until it starts to brown, then add the garlic and cook for another minute.

Add the black beans and chipotles to the pot and stir through the coriander. Cover the beans with enough water to reach 2.5cm (1in) above the beans, and bring to the boil. Reduce heat to low, uncover, and simmer for an hour.

Stir through the salt and lime juice and leave to simmer until the beans are completely tender – they should crumble in your fingers. To thicken, use a potato masher to crush some of the beans or run a stick blender through the pot for 20 seconds.

Serve beans as nachos (see Slow Cooked Stuff) or crumble Mexican white cheese (queso fresco, or any other white cheese like fetta) and chopped coriander over the top to serve as a side.

BLACK BEANS

SWEET BARBECUE BEANS

**Start this recipe 2 hours before you want to eat it |
Serves 8**

These beans are great with meat, they're also good *instead*
of meat! Vegetarians can enjoy a barbecue as well as
carnivores.

2 tablespoons butter
1 brown onion, finely
 chopped
1 garlic clove, finely
 chopped
1 cup ketchup or tomato
 sauce
¼ cup brown sugar

2 tablespoons treacle
2 tablespoons maple syrup
2 tablespoons cider vinegar
1 tablespoon American
 mustard
2 x 400g (14oz) cans
 kidney beans, drained
 and rinsed

In a large pot over medium heat, melt the butter and sauté
the onions for 5 minutes. Add the garlic and cook for
another minute. Add the ketchup, brown sugar, treacle,
maple syrup, vinegar and mustard; stir. Bring to the boil.

 Reduce the heat and simmer mixture for five minutes.
Add the beans and stir. Cover with a lid, and cook for
five minutes. Uncover and leave to simmer for another 10
minutes, until thickened.

Start this recipe 4 hours before you want to eat it | Serves 8

These soft, delicious pinto beans are essential for nachos and burritos.

4 cups dried pinto beans
1 tablespoon olive oil
1 white onion, finely chopped
2 garlic cloves, finely chopped
1 pickled jalapeño, finely chopped
2 teaspoons cumin
1 tablespoon salt

Clean and rinse pinto beans. Place beans in a large pot, then pour over enough water to reach 5cm (2ins) above the beans. Cover, and set aside overnight to soak. Alternatively, bring the pot to the boil and cook for 15 minutes, cover, reduce heat and simmer beans for an hour. Drain the beans and set aside.

In another large pot, warm oil over medium heat. Add the onion and cook for 5 minutes until it starts to brown, then add garlic and cook for another minute.

Add the pinto beans to the pot with the pickled jalapeño. Stir through the cumin. Cover the beans with enough water to reach 2.5cm (1in) above the beans, and bring to the boil. Reduce heat to low, uncover, and simmer for an hour.

Stir through the salt and leave the pan to simmer until the beans are completely tender – they should crumble in your fingers. To thicken, use a potato masher to crush some of the beans or run a stick blender through the pot for 20 seconds.

PINTO BEANS

PULLED PORK NACHOS

Start this recipe 1 hour before you want to eat it | Serves 4

These nachos are the most popular thing on the menu. They're a big plate of Tex-Mex goodness, and great way to use up any leftover pulled pork after a barbecue. 'Leftover pulled pork' is usually an oxymoron, but you never know!

200g (7oz) good quality unsalted corn chips
4 cups Pulled Pork (see Slow Cooked Stuff)
2 cups Pinto Beans
2 cups grated cheddar cheese
2 cups Tomato Salsa (see Sauces, Salsa, Salads & Sides)

½ cup Jalapeño Cream (see Sauces, Salsa, Salads & Sides)
¼ cup Barbecue Sauce (see Sauces, Salsa, Salads & Sides)
2 tablespoons coriander (cilantro), finely chopped
2 tablespoons spring onion (eschallots), finely chopped
4 large heat-proof plates

Preheat the oven to 180°C/350°F.

Scatter two handfuls of corn chips over each plate. Arrange the corn chips neatly around the edges so it looks like a sun.

Using tongs, scatter a cup of pulled pork over the middle of the chips on each plate. Spoon half a cup of Pinto Beans over the pork.

Sprinkle a big handful of cheese over each plate and pop them into the oven for 15 minutes, until the cheese is melted and golden.

Remove the plates from the oven and spoon half a cup of Tomato Salsa over the cheese, down the middle of each plate.

Using a sauce bottle, squeeze a zig zag of Jalapeño Cream over the salsa. Make another zig zag with the Barbecue Sauce.

Sprinkle coriander and spring onions over the top of each plate of nachos and serve immediately.

DOUBLE BEAN NACHOS

Start this recipe 1 hour before you want to eat it | Serves 4

The combination of not one, but two – that's right, two – kinds of beans makes these Double Bean Nachos delicious.

200g (7oz) good quality, unsalted corn chips
2 cups Black Beans
2 cups Pinto Beans
2 cups grated cheddar cheese
2 cups Tomato Salsa (see Sauces, Salsas, Salads & Sides)

½ cup Jalapeño Cream (see Sauces, Salsas, Salads & Sides)
2 tablespoons coriander (cilantro), finely chopped
2 tablespoons spring onion (eschallots), finely chopped
4 large heat-proof plates

Preheat the oven to 180°C/350°F.

Scatter two handfuls of corn chips over each plate. Arrange the corn chips neatly around the edges so it looks like a sun.

Spoon half a cup of Black Beans across the plate, over the chips. Spoon half a cup of Pinto Beans right next to the black beans.

Sprinkle a big handful of cheese over each plate and pop them into the oven for 15 minutes, until the cheese is melted and golden on top.

Remove the plates from the oven and spoon half a cup of Tomato Salsa down the middle of each plate, over the cheese.

Using a sauce bottle, squeeze a zig zag of Jalapeño Cream over the salsa. Sprinkle coriander and spring onions over the top of each plate of nachos and serve immediately.

BEEF SHORT RIB NACHOS

Start this recipe 1 hour before you want to eat it | Serves 4

I realised that the only way to improve one of the world's greatest foods (beef short ribs) braised in two of the world's greatest drinks (beer and cola) was to pile it on top of another of the world's greatest foods (corn chips) and cover the whole thing with yet another of the world's greatest foods (cheese!).

200g (7oz) good quality, unsalted corn chips
4 cups shredded Beef Short Ribs
2 cups grated cheddar cheese
2 cups Tomato Salsa (see Sauces, Salsas, Salads & Sides)
½ cup Jalapeño Cream (see Sauces, Salsas, Salads & Sides)
2 tablespoon coriander (cilantro), finely chopped
2 tablespoons spring onion (eschallots), finely chopped
4 large heat-proof plates

Preheat the oven to 180°C/350°F.

Scatter two handfuls of corn chips over each plate. Arrange the corn chips neatly around the edges so it looks like a sun.

Use tongs to scatter a cup of shredded Beef Short Ribs over the middle of the chips on each plate.

Sprinkle a big handful of cheese over each plate and pop them into the oven for 15 minutes, until the cheese is melted and golden on top.

Remove the plates from the oven and spoon half a cup of Tomato Salsa down the middle of each plate, over the cheese.

Using a sauce bottle squirt a zig zag of Jalapeño Cream over the salsa. Sprinkle coriander and spring onions over the top of each plate of nachos and serve immediately.

BURGERS & SANDWICHES

TIPS FOR

HAMBURGER GREATNESS

1. MINCE YOUR OWN BEEF. Get a big fatty piece of chuck, cut it into cubes and run it through a mincer. They're not too expensive and freshly minced meat just tastes that much better.

2. USE GOOD QUALITY BURGER BUNS and either steam them for a soft warm bun or throw them on the grill for a great charred flavour.

3. MAKE THE MEAT PATTY THE SAME WIDTH AS THE BUN. If you make them too big the burgers will be hard to eat. Make them too small and everyone will hate you. You want the patties the same width as the bun. Use a ruler to measure them if you have to.

4. ONCE THE MEAT IS ON THE GRILL DON'T PRESS IT! Flip it once or twice but don't press down on it! You don't wanna lose all the awesome juices and have a dry, flavourless burger.

5. DON'T OVERCOOK THE MEAT. Leave it a little pink on the inside at the very least. If you're buying your own fresh beef you should enjoy it nice and red.

CLASSIC CHEESEBURGER

The best cheeseburgers are simple, cheesy and pickly. If you are mincing the meat yourself, use steak with around 20 per cent fat. Whatever you do, don't put breadcrumbs or vegetables through your beef patties. It's sacrilege!

500g (1lb) beef mince
salt
1 tablespoon butter
1 white onion, sliced into rings
1 teaspoon brown sugar
1 tablespoon olive oil
4 slices sharp cheddar cheese
4 good quality burger buns

2 dill pickles, sliced (see Sauces, Salsas, Salads & Sides)
ketchup or tomato sauce
American mustard

Place the mince in a mixing bowl and knead it into four burger patties. Place the burger patties on a plate and lightly salt them. Leave them to sit for 20 minutes to reach room temperature.

Melt the butter in a pan over low heat. Add the onion and cook, uncovered, for 15 minutes, stirring the pan every minute to make sure the onions don't stick to the bottom. Once the onions are nice and soft add the brown sugar and cook for another 10 minutes, until the onions are sticky and browned. Remove from heat and set aside.

Boil a pan of water over high heat, and place a steamer over the pan.

Coat a medium hot barbecue hot plate or large frying pan with olive oil. Add burger patties and cook on one side for two minutes.

Flip each burger patty and place a slice of cheese on top of each of them. Let the cheese melt while you cook each patty for another 2 minutes. Remove the patties from the hot plate and keep them warm.

Halve each bun and place in the steamer and steam for 1–2 minutes until soft and fluffy. Transfer the buns to a plate.

On the bottom half of each bun place two pickle slices and a spoonful of the caramelized onion. Place a beef patty on top of the pickles and onions. Smear some ketchup and mustard on the other half of the bun and place it on top.

BURGER WITH THE LOT

Start this recipe 1 hour before you want to eat it | Makes 4 burgers

The quintessential 'works' burger with everything; a staple of any burger joint worth visiting. Best washed down with a milkshake — my fave is lime — your reward after managing to squeeze this monster into your mouth.

500g (1lb) beef mince
salt
2 tablespoons olive oil
4 slices sharp cheddar cheese
4 rashers smoked bacon
4 eggs
1 white onion, sliced into rings
4 rings canned pineapple

4 good quality burger buns
4 tablespoons whole egg mayonnaise
¼ iceberg lettuce, shredded
1 tomato, sliced
4 slices canned beetroot
4 tablespoons Barbecue Sauce (see
    Sauces, Salsas, Salads & Sides)

Place the mince in a mixing bowl and knead it into four burger patties. Place the burger patties on a plate and lightly salt them. Leave them to sit for 20 minutes to reach room temperature.

Coat a medium hot barbecue hot plate or large frying pan with 1 tablespoon olive oil. Turn griller on to high. You can either do all the cooking at once or one thing at a time, just make sure to keep everything warm.

Cook one side of the patties on the hot plate for 2 minutes. Flip each burger patty and place a slice of cheese on top. Let the cheese melt while you cook each patty for another two minutes. Remove the patties from the hot plate and keep them warm.

Fry the bacon on the hot plate for one minute on each side. Set aside and keep warm.

Crack each egg onto the hot plate and fry it sunny side up for 2 minutes, keeping yolk runny. Use a metal spatula to make sure the eggs don't combine. Once cooked, set aside and keep warm.

Cook the onions on the hot plate in remaining olive oil. Flip them after 2 minutes and remove them once they start to char a little.

Grill the pineapple slices for 1 minute on each side.

Halve the buns and toast each half on the grill for 10 seconds on each side.

To assemble burgers, spread some mayonnaise on the bottom half of each bun, then layer on top: lettuce, a few onion rings, a tomato slice, beetroot, grilled pineapple, a beef patty topped with cheese, a slice of bacon and a fried egg, sunny side up. Spoon Barbecue Sauce on the other half of each bun, place on burger and serve.

FRIED CHICKEN BURGER

Start this recipe 1 hour before you want to eat it | Makes 4 burgers

This chicken burger is so perfectly crunchy, spicy and chickeny. Good vibes ahoy.

4 chicken thigh fillets, skin on
1 cup buttermilk
2 cups plain flour
½ teaspoon salt
½ teaspoon black pepper
½ teaspoon cayenne pepper
4 good quality burger buns
1 cup finely chopped iceberg lettuce
½ cup Chipotle Mayo (see Sauces,
    Salsas, Salads & Sides)
2 tablespoons finely chopped
    coriander (cilantro)

Place the chicken thighs in a bowl and cover them with the buttermilk. Place chicken and milk in the fridge for 30 minutes.

In a large plastic container, combine the flour, salt and peppers. Add the chicken thighs, put the lid on the container and shake until the chicken is evenly coated.

Heat cooking oil in a deep fryer or frying pan to 140°C/280°F and add the chicken. Cook for 15–20 minutes, until the batter coating the chicken is deep yellow in colour. Remove the chicken from the oil and set aside.

Boil a pan of water over high heat, and place a steamer over the pan. Increase the deep fryer or frying pan heat to 180°C/350°F. Fry chicken for 2–3 minutes, until golden brown. The batter should be nice and crispy.

Transfer the chicken to paper towels to soak up the excess oil.

Halve each bun and place in the steamer. Let them steam for 2 minutes until soft, hot and fluffy. Remove from steamer.

To assemble, scatter some iceberg lettuce on the bottom half of each bun and squeeze some Chipotle Mayo on the top half. Place a chicken thigh over the lettuce and scatter some coriander over the chicken. Place the top half of the bun on top of the chicken thigh and serve.

WATERMELON & BACON BURGER

Start this recipe 90 minutes before you want to eat it | Makes 6 burgers

Before I opened my own place, I worked a couple of shifts with my 'real chef' pals Mitch and Limbo. My fave dish of theirs was a grilled piece of watermelon, served with herbs and vegetables in lime and garlic oil. It was a simple and flavorsome dish and I always wondered what it would be like served as a sandwich. I started making watermelon burgers, topped with a rasher of bacon, and they sold like hotcakes. Thanks to Mitch and Limbo for the inspiration. Sorry about all those plates I broke.

¼ seedless watermelon
1 cup Lime Vinaigrette (see Sauces, Salsas, Salads & Sides)
12 rashers smoked bacon
1 white onion, sliced into rings
1 cup Lime Mayo (see Sauces, Salsas, Salads & Sides)
1 bunch of rocket (arugula), washed6 good quality burger buns
6 good quality burger buns

Using a knife, remove the watermelon rind. Cut the watermelon into 3cm (1¼ins) thick slices.

Cook each piece of watermelon on a hot char-grill or barbecue for 2 minutes on each side, until dark grill lines are visible.

Place each piece of watermelon in a bowl and cover with the Lime Vinaigrette. Leave to sit for at least an hour.

Light the hot plate on your barbecue and crank it up high. Cook the bacon for one minute on each side; and do the same with the onion rings Don't be afraid to char the onions a little. Place the watermelon slices back on the char-grill and cook for two minutes a side.

Halve the burger buns and toast, cut side down, on the char-grill, or under a heated griller, for 10 seconds on each side.

Place a few onion rings on the bottom half of each bun and a few leaves of rocket. Then layer a watermelon slice and two slices of bacon. Smear some of the Lime Mayo on the top half of each bun and place on top of the burger. You might need to use a skewer to hold each burger together.

Start this recipe 30 minutes before you want to eat it | Makes 4 sandwiches

The Southern Smoke is my attempt at recreating that first pulled pork sandwich I had in Memphis when I was a kid. It gets its name from a series of Southern rap mix-tapes by DJ Smallz called *Southern Smoke*. If you put one of these awesome mixes on at a barbecue, the food will taste better. These are best made as soon as you've pulled the pork from the shoulder, when it's piping hot and fresh. I normally have 50 little rolls, a big pan of beans and a bowl of slaw and everyone makes their own sandwiches. If you have vegetarian guests hold the pork and give them a roll with beans and slaw – it's almost as good!

4 soft white rolls or baps
4 cups hot Pulled Pork (see Slow Cooked Stuff)
4 tablespoons Barbecue Sauce (see Sauces, Salsas, Salads & Sides)
2 cups hot Sweet Barbecue Beans (see Slow Cooked Stuff)
2 cups Cabbage & Apple Slaw (see Sauces, Salsas, Salads & Sides)
4 dill pickles, to serve (see Sauces, Salsas, Salads & Sides)

Bring a large pan of water to the boil over high heat. Place a steamer over the pan of water and steam the rolls for 1–2 minutes until they're hot and fluffy.

Transfer the rolls to a plate and place one cup of Pulled Pork in each roll. Spoon some Barbecue Sauce over the pork.

Place half a cup of beans on top of the pork and half a cup of slaw on top of the beans. Place the top of the roll on the sandwich. Serve with a dill pickle on the side.

SOUTHERN SMOKE

PULLED PORK BANH MI

Start this recipe 1 hour before you want to eat it | Makes 1 baguette, serves 6

It's a fact that the Vietnamese 'banh mi' is the ultimate sandwich. There's not much Asian influence in the other recipes in here, but I eat so many banh mis that I had to pay homage to it. This is a different way of serving pulled pork, and is perfect for parties or big gatherings. Banh mis are made on baguettes, which are then cut into smaller sandwiches, held together with skewers. If you wanna just serve one long sandwich, that's cool too. Our record for most banh mi baguettes assembled at one party is 25. See if you can beat that.

2 carrots, peeled
1 daikon radish, peeled
2 tablespoons sugar
½ teaspoon salt
1 cup white vinegar
1 baguette
100g (3½oz) pork paté
¼ cup whole egg mayonnaise

1 telegraph cucumber, thinly sliced lengthwise with a mandoline
4 spring onions (eschallots), ends removed
½ cup coriander (cilantro) sprigs
4 cups hot Pulled Pork (see zzz)
2 bird's eye chilies, finely chopped
6 wooden skewers

Using a mandoline, cut the carrots and radish into matchsticks. Place them in a plastic container and sprinkle the sugar and salt over the top. Add the vinegar and 1 cup warm water and seal the container. Refrigerate for at least 24 hours, or up to a week.

Slice one side of a baguette lengthwise, from one end to the other, but do not cut completely in half. Open it flat and spread the paté on the bottom and the mayonnaise on top.

Lay the slices of cucumber over the mayo and place the spring onions down the middle of the baguette. Spread the pickled carrots and daikon over the cucumber. Scatter the coriander over, followed by the pork. Scatter the chilies over the pork and close the baguette.

Push 6 skewers through the baguette, leaving 10cm (4ins) or so between each skewer. Use a bread knife to divide the baguette into 6 sandwiches.

Start this recipe 30 minutes before you want to eat it | Makes 4 sandwiches

One of the elusive sandwiches on the menu at 'Krusty Burger' from *The Simpsons* cartoon. My friends and I used to joke about making a pork rib sandwich, but cutting all the bones out of pork ribs seemed too fiddly. The braised beef short ribs, however, are perfect for placing between two slices of bread, or on a crusty roll.

1 large red capsicum (bell pepper), quartered, core and seeds removed
1 tablespoon butter
1 Spanish (purple) onion, sliced into rings
1 teaspoon brown sugar
4 crusty bread rolls

¼ cup whole egg mayonnaise
4 cups hot Beef Short Ribs (see Slow Cooked Stuff)
4 slices provolone cheese
4 Dill Pickles, to serve (see Sauces, Salsas, Salads & Sides)

Bring your barbecue grill or char-grill pan to high heat and grill the capsicum, skin side down, until the skin is black and charred. Remove from the grill and place the capsicum in a sealed plastic bag and leave it to sweat for 15 minutes.

Remove the capsicum from the bag and peel off the blackened skin. Set the capsicum to one side.

Melt the butter in a pan over low heat. Add the onion and cook, uncovered, for 15 minutes, stirring often to make sure the onions don't stick to the bottom of the pan. Once the onions are nice and soft add the sugar and cook for another 10 minutes, until the onions are sticky and browned. Remove from heat and set aside.

Cut the rolls in half lengthwise and spread with mayonnaise. Add 1 cup of the Beef Short Ribs to each roll and top with a slice of cheese, some onions and a piece of capsicum. Place the top of the roll on the sandwich and serve with a dill pickle on the side.

RIBWICH

FRIED OYSTER PO BOY

Straight out of New Orleans, Louisiana, the Oyster Po Boy is a simple and hearty sandwich. I recommend buying extra oysters because you will probably eat a stack of them before they make it onto your sandwich.

20 oysters, shucked and cleaned
1½ cups milk
2 eggs, lightly beaten
1 cup plain flour
1 cup cornmeal
2 teaspoons salt
1 teaspoon freshly cracked black pepper

½ teaspoon cayenne pepper
4 soft long bread rolls
2 cups finely shredded iceberg lettuce
½ lemon
½ cup Lime Mayo (see Sauces, Salsas, Salads & Sides)
Tabasco or hot sauce

Place the oysters in a bowl and cover with one cup of milk. Leave to sit for 20 minutes.

Combine ½ cup of milk and the eggs in a bowl.

In a plastic container with a lid, combine the flour, cornmeal, salt, pepper and cayenne pepper, making sure all the dry ingredients mix thoroughly.

Remove the oysters from the milk and drain. In batches of five at a time, dip the oysters in the egg mixture and then add them to the plastic container with the flour. Place the lid on the container and shake until the oysters are coated evenly. Repeat with remaining oysters.

Heat cooking oil in your deep fryer or frying pan to 180°C/350°F. Fry the oysters in batches of five for 3 minutes, until golden brown. Repeat for the rest of the oysters, transferring them to paper towel after frying to absorb any excess oil.

Cut the rolls lengthwise, and place half a cup of the lettuce on the bottom half of the roll. Top the lettuce with five fried oysters and squeeze lemon juice over the top. Drizzle with lime mayo and hot sauce to taste.

POACHED SHRIMP ROLL

These classy little sandwiches are perfect for Sunday afternoons. The shrimps are poached in tea and covered in a herbed mayo before you cram them into a roll with avocado and butter lettuce. Delish.

20 shrimp (prawns), uncooked
4 cups brewed black tea, room temperature
salt
½ cup whole egg mayonnaise
juice of one lemon
1 tablespoon mint, finely chopped
1 tablespoon tarragon, finely chopped
1 tablespoon chives, finely chopped
1 teaspoon freshly cracked black pepper
4 brioche rolls
butter
8 butter lettuce leaves
½ avocado, thinly sliced

Peel shrimp, leaving tails intact. Place the shrimp in a pan over medium heat, and pour in the black tea to cover. Season with salt. Cook for 6 minutes until the liquid is almost boiling, and remove from heat. Be careful not to overcook the shrimp. Remove shrimp from the pan and set them aside to cool. In a mixing bowl, combine the mayonnaise and lemon juice. Add the shrimp and chopped herbs to the bowl and stir well to combine.

Place a frying pan on the stove over high heat. Halve rolls lengthwise and spread with butter. Toast the rolls in the pan for 10 seconds a side, and transfer to a plate.

Place two lettuce leaves and two slices of avocado on the bottom half of each roll. Top with five shrimp, drizzling any leftover mayonnaise mixture over the top.

GRILLED MAC & CHEESE SANDWICH

Start this recipe 5 minutes before you want to eat it | Makes 1 sandwich

This recipe is the reason you will always make double the Mac & Cheese you need. Everyone likes a grilled cheese sandwich but a Grilled Mac & Cheese Sandwich is as good as it gets.

leftover Mac & Cheese (see Sauces, Salsas, Salads & Sides)
two slices of white bread
butter

Place a heavy based frying pan over medium heat.

Butter one side of each slice of bread. Spoon a generous serve of Mac & Cheese over the unbuttered side of one piece of bread and place the other slice on top, butter side up.

Place the sandwich in the pan and cook for two minutes, until the bread is golden. Flip the sandwich and grill the other side until golden.

Cut into triangles and serve.

Start this recipe 5 minutes before you want to eat it | Makes 1 sandwich

Welcome to the dumbest recipe in the whole book. When I used to DJ a lot I would travel to some weird country towns, flying in that evening, going straight to the gig and usually missing dinner. By the time the gig was over, everything in town would be closed. The hotels I stayed in were generally just a room with a bed, a bible and an iron. So I taught myself how to cook a grilled cheese sandwich with an iron, just like Johnny Depp did in the movie *Benny & Joon*. If you ever find yourself in a similar situation, or you just wanna impress some other idiot, this is the recipe for you!

2 slices of bread
2 slices of cheddar cheese
butter
aluminium foil
an iron

Butter both sides of each slice of bread and place the cheese in the middle. Wrap the sandwich in aluminium foil.

Empty the iron of any water and set it to its highest setting. Place the foil wrapped sandwich on the ironing board.

Press the iron flat onto one side of the foil. Hold it there for 30 seconds to a minute. Unwrap the foil a little to make sure the bread is toasted to your liking.

Flip the sandwich over and press the iron down on the other side for 30 seconds to a minute. Turn off the iron.

Carefully unwrap the sandwich from the foil and enjoy! Then speak to your agent about booking you less of these weird small town shows.

IRONED CHEESE SANDWICH

HOT DOGS

WELCOME TO THE HOT DOG SECTION.

I love hot dogs so much that I have some rules you must abide by:

1. ONLY USE KOSHER FRANKFURTS. They are 100 per cent beef, smoked and delicious. They grill better than pork frankfurts and are a nicer, much redder colour. Try getting them from a kosher butcher or in the kosher section of the supermarket.

2. GRILL YOUR FRANKFURTS. It tastes better and by not boiling them you avoid one of the worst things about hot dogs: the dreaded hot dog-flavoured water

3. STEAM YOUR BUNS. It makes the entire dog nice and warm and the pillowy bread makes the whole thing easier to eat. We have brioche hot dog buns made specially for our dawgs, so try to find something similar.

4. AMERICAN MUSTARD. Every hot dog needs a squiggle of American mustard down the middle. Hot dogs just look and taste better with that squiggle of mustard. It's essential.

Ok those are the rules...it's dawg time!

Start this recipe 1 hour before you want to eat it | Makes 4 hot dogs

The original and maybe the best dawg I ever came up with. Lev's Dawg is kinda Mexican with a nice stripe of chipotle mayo down the middle and some tomato salsa on top, but there's some pickled grilled yellow peppers on there to keep things multi-regional. This is a good dog – so good I had to name it after me, if only to constantly hear my name being mispronounced by drunk people ordering it.

2 banana capsicums (yellow peppers)
2 tablespoons rice wine vinegar
2 teaspoons olive oil
1 tablespoon sugar
1 teaspoon salt
4 kosher frankfurts

4 good quality hot dog buns
¼ cup Chipotle Mayo (see Sauces, Salsas, Salads & Sides)
1 cup Tomato Salsa (see Sauces, Salsas, Salads & Sides)
American mustard

Heat a barbecue or char-grill pan to high. Wash the banana capsicums and cut off the stalks. Grill them until black on all sides. Chop them finely or process in a food processor until chunky.

Place the chopped capsicums in a bowl and stir through the rice wine vinegar, olive oil, sugar and salt until well combined. Set aside.

Fill a large pan with water and place a steamer over the top. Bring it to a rolling boil over high heat.

Grill frankfurts lengthwise across the grill until they start to char. Turn regularly to ensure they're cooked evenly.

Cut the buns lengthwise, leaving 1cm (½in) of bread at the bottom of the roll. Steam the buns in the steamer for 2 minutes until soft and piping hot.

Spread some Chipotle Mayo along the bottom of each bun. Place a grilled frankfurt in each bun. Spoon some Tomato Salsa on one side of each bun, next to the frankfurt. Spoon a smaller amount of the pickled capsicums over the other side. Squirt a zig zag of mustard over the top of each hot dog and serve.

LEV'S DAWG

Start this recipe 1 hour before you want to eat it | Makes 4 hot dogs

The Big Windy is my take on the classic Chicago hot dog. To be totally legitimate you should use hot dog buns topped with poppy seeds, if you can find them. While you eat it you should re-enact scenes from *Ferris Bueller's Day Off* while listening to juke.

10 spiced gherkins
10 mini cocktail onions
green food colouring
4 kosher frankfurts
4 good quality hot dog buns
  (preferably topped with poppy seeds)
2 Dill Pickles (see Sauces, Salsas,
  Salads & Sides), cut lengthwise into
spears
1 tomato, halved and sliced
4 sport peppers or pickled mild yellow
  peppers
¼ white onion, finely diced
celery salt
American mustard

Place the spiced gherkins and the cocktail onions in a food processor and blend until smooth. Add three drops of food colouring and stir until the relish mixture is bright green.

Fill a large pan with water and place a steamer on top. Bring it to a rolling boil over high heat.

Heat a barbecue or char-grill pan to high. Grill the frankfurts lengthwise across the grill until they start to char. Turn regularly to ensure they're cooking evenly.

Cut the buns lengthwise, leaving 1cm (½in) of bread at the bottom of the roll. Steam the buns in the steamer for 2 minutes until soft and piping hot.

Place a grilled frankfurt in each steamed bun and place two pickle spears next to it. On the other side of each bun place two slices of tomato. Place a sport pepper on each frankfurt and scatter some white onion over the top. Spoon some of the neon green relish over the onion and sprinkle with a pinch of celery salt.

Squirt a zig zag of mustard over each dog and serve.

BIG WINDY

DYNAMITE CHILI DAWG

Start this recipe 1 hour before you want to eat it | Makes 4 hot dogs

I named this dawg after Captain Franco and Count Doyle, who ran a reggae and soul party called Dynamite!

4 kosher frankfurts
4 good quality hot dog buns
2 cups hot Dynamite Beef Chili (see Slow Cooked Stuff)
¼ white onion, finely diced

50g (1¾oz) Mexican white cheese (Queso Fresco, or any other white cheese, like fetta)
American mustard

Fill a large pan with water and place a steamer on top. Bring it to a rolling boil over high heat.

Heat a barbecue or char-grill pan to high. Grill the frankfurts lengthwise across the grill until they start to char. Turn regularly to ensure they're cooking evenly.

Cut the buns lengthwise, leaving 1cm (½in) of bread at the bottom of the roll. Steam the buns in the steamer for 2 minutes until soft and piping hot.

Place a grilled frankfurt in each bun and spoon half a cup of beef chili over the frankfurt lengthwise. Sprinkle some chopped white onion over the top. Grate some white cheese over the onion. Finish each dog with a zig zag of mustard and serve.

Start this recipe 1 hour before you want to eat it | Makes 4 hot dogs

The full name of this hot dog is 'The Ro Sham Bo Confuse Di Mouth Commemorative Cheeseburger Dawg'. It's a bigger mouthful to say than it is to eat! A couple of years back, I started a DJ crew called Ro Sham Bo. Since we played a wildly diverse range of music our motto was 'confuse di dance'. When we put on the last ever Ro Sham Bo party I made up this hot dog as a tribute. The dance confusion may be over, but the mouth confusion will live on forever with a hot dog that tastes like a cheeseburger!

4 kosher frankfurts
4 good quality hot dog buns
200g (7oz) cheddar cheese, grated
2 Dill Pickles (see Sauces, Salsas,
    Salads & Sides), cut lengthwise into
    spears

¼ white onion, finely diced
ketchup (or tomato sauce)
American mustard

Fill a large pan with water and place a steamer on top. Bring it to a rolling boil over high heat.

Heat a barbecue or char-grill pan to high. Grill the frankfurts lengthwise across the grill until they start to char. Turn regularly to ensure they're cooking evenly.

Cut the buns lengthwise, leaving 1cm (½ in) of bread at the bottom of the roll.

Stuff 60g (2oz) of cheese into each bun and place them in the steamer. Steam the buns for 2 minutes until the cheese has completely melted.

Place a grilled frankfurt over the cheese in each bun. On one side of the bun, place two pickle spears next to the frankfurt and sprinkle some chopped white onion on the other. Squirt a zig zag of ketchup over the hot dog, followed by a zig zag of mustard, and serve.

CONFUSE DI MOUTH

Start this recipe 1 hour before you want to eat it | Makes 4 hot dogs

We featured this dog on our menu as a special to celebrate Chilean Independence Day, at the request of one of the three Chilean people we know. The Completo is how they do hot dogs in Chile – with sauerkraut, mashed avocado and mayonnaise.

2 avocados
1 tablespoon lime juice
4 kosher frankfurts
4 good quality hot dog buns
½ cup sauerkraut
½ cup Lime Mayo (see Sauces, Salsas,
    Salads & Sides)

Place the avocado flesh in a food processor and blend until smooth. Add the lime juice and blend for another 20 seconds.

Fill a large pan with water and place a steamer on top. Bring it to a rolling boil over high heat.

Heat a barbecue or char-grill pan to high. Grill the frankfurts lengthwise across the grill until they start to char. Turn regularly to ensure they're cooking evenly.

Cut the buns lengthwise, leaving 1cm (½in) of bread at the bottom of the roll. Steam the buns in the steamer for 2 minutes until soft and piping hot.

Spread a tablespoon of sauerkraut in the bottom of each bun. Place a frankfurt on top and spoon some blended avocado over, ensuring the frankfurt is completely covered by avocado. Squirt a zig zag of Lime Mayo over the top of each hot dog and serve.

THE COMPLETO

PICKLZ'N SLAW DAWG

Start this recipe 1 hour before you want to eat it | Makes 4 hot dogs

A simple and tasty dawg, pickles and coleslaw on top of a frankfurt with a squiggle of mustard. I spell 'picklz' with a Z because that's how all the kids are doing it these days.

4 kosher frankfurts
4 good quality hot dog buns
2 Dill Pickles (see Sauces, Salsas,
    Salads & Sides), cut into spears
2 cups Apple & Cabbage Slaw (see
    Sauces, Salsas, Salads & Sides)
American mustard

Fill a large pan with water and place a steamer on top. Bring it to a rolling boil over high heat.

Heat a barbecue or char-grill pan to high. Grill the frankfurts lengthwise across the grill until they start to char. Turn regularly to ensure they're cooking evenly.

Cut the buns lengthwise, leaving 1 cm (½in) of bread at the bottom of the roll. Steam the buns in the steamer for 2 minutes until soft and piping hot.

Place a grilled frankfurt inside each bun and place two pickle spears on either side. Using tongs, place half a cup of the slaw over each frankfurt. Finish each dog with a zig zag of mustard over the top.

Start this recipe 1 hour before you want to eat it | Makes 4 hot dogs

This dog, topped with black beans and yellow mustard, was named after the rapper Wiz Khalifa, who released a big hit, *Black and Yellow*, a few years ago.

4 kosher frankfurts
4 good quality hot dog buns
½ cup sour cream
2 cups Black Beans (see Sauces,
   Salsas, Salads & Sides)
American mustard

Fill a large pan with water and place a steamer on top. Bring it to a rolling boil over high heat.

Heat a barbecue or char-grill pan to high. Grill the frankfurts lengthwise across the grill until they start to char. Turn regularly to ensure they're cooking evenly.

Cut the buns lengthwise, leaving 1cm (½in) of bread at the bottom of the roll. Steam the buns in the steamer for 2 minutes until soft and piping hot.

Spread a tablespoon of sour cream over the bottom of each bun and place a grilled frankfurt on op. Spoon half a cup of the black beans over each frankfurt. Squirt a zig zag of mustard over the top of the black beans and serve.

THE WIZ KHALIFA

SAUCES, SALSAS, SALADS & SIDES

Start this recipe 15 minutes before you want to eat it. Makes 3 cups

This zesty little cream is a spicier alternative to guacamole, and great for dipping corn chips into with salsa. It's also awesome on top of nachos.

2 heaped tablespoons of pickled
   jalapeño chilies
1 avocado
2 cups sour cream
1 tablespoon of finely chopped
   coriander (cilantro)
1 tablespoon of lime juice
1 pinch of salt

Place the pickled jalapeños into a food processor (or blender) and process until the jalapeños become a smooth green paste.

   Add the avocado and process until smooth. Add the sour cream, coriander, lime juice and salt and process for another minute until combined. Keeps covered in refrigerator for 3 days.

JALAPEÑO CREAM

LEV'S DAWG'S OWN BARBECUE SAUCE

Start this recipe 90 minutes before you want to eat it | Makes 5 cups

I've spent years trying to perfect my barbecue sauce. This one is good and sweet, with a nice vinegar kick. We started bottling it and when I first saw the label with my name on it I felt a pride so deep that I'll probably never feel it again until I have a son old enough to bottle his own barbecue sauce with his name on it.

2 tablespoons of butter	1 cup brown sugar
1 white onion	½ cup mustard
2 cloves of garlic	½ cup ketchup
1 teaspoon cayenne pepper	1 cup cider vinegar
450g (16oz) of treacle (or molasses)	1 cup orange juice
	½ cup Worcestershire sauce

In a large pot melt the butter over low heat. Add the onions and sauté them until just brown, about two minutes. Add the garlic and cook for another minute. Stir in the cayenne pepper and mustard and cook for two minutes.

Add the rest of the ingredients and stir. Increase the heat to high and bring to the boil for one minute. Turn the heat back down to low and let the pot simmer, uncovered, for an hour.

Remove from the heat and allow the sauce to cool before putting it over everything in existence. Keeps for two weeks in the fridge.

SPICY BARBECUE SAUCE

This is a very thin, runny sauce that's perfect for using as a mop on a big piece of meat in the smoker. Just slop some on the meat every hour or so and let the sauce work its sweet and spicy magic.

2 cups cider vinegar
1 tablespoon brown sugar
2 tablespoons red chili
   flakes
1 tablespoons salt
1 teaspoon black pepper
1 teaspoon paprika

Place all ingredients in a pan and bring to boil. Reduce heat to low and simmer for 15 minutes. Allow sauce to cool before using. Keeps forever in the fridge.

Start this recipe 15 minutes before you want to eat it | Makes 3 cups, enough for one squeezy sauce bottle full

Ranch is essential for Hot Wings and works well as a salad dressing. My Ranch has a lot of herbs in it. It almost tastes healthy but it definitely is not.

½ cup finely chopped chives
¼ cup finely chopped coriander
  (cilantro)
¼ cup finely chopped mint
1½ cups whole egg mayonnaise
1½ cups sour cream
1 tablespoon lime juice
1 pinch of salt
1 teaspoon black pepper

Place all the ingredients in a bowl and stir until combined. Add more lime juice and salt to taste.

Ranch dressing can also be made in a food processor or blender – just throw everything in and mince it up together. Keeps for 3 days in the fridge.

RANCH DRESSING

Start this recipe 5 minutes before you want to eat it | Makes 1 cup

One super-important rule is to always use whole egg mayonnaise. Always – no excuses! All other kinds are rotten. We use Hellman's, S&W is great, and I have a soft spot for Paul Newman's mayonnaise too.
This spicy mayonnaise is addictive, and goes well with everything. Chipotles in adobo are smoked jalapeño peppers in tomato sauce. They're available in most supermarkets, and online.

1 cup whole egg mayonnaise
¼ cup chipotles in adobo

Add chipotles in adobo to food processor and blend until smooth. Add the mayo and continue blending until combined.

CHIPOTLE MAYO

LIME MAYO

Start this recipe 5 minutes before you want to eat it | Makes 1 cup

It's pretty simple – lime juice and mayonnaise. But it's unbelievably good slathered over grilled corn.

2 tablespoons lime juice
1 cup whole egg mayonnaise

In a bowl, stir the lime juice into the mayonnaise until combined.

DILL MAYO

Start this recipe 5 minutes before you want to eat it | Makes 1 cup

Dill is an underrated little herb. This mayo is great on burgers! But it's unbelievably good slathered over grilled corn.

¼ cup finely chopped dill
1 cup whole egg mayonnaise

In a bowl, stir the dill into the mayonnaise until combined.

Start this recipe 5 minutes before you want to eat it | Makes 1 cup

This simple vinaigrette is great to keep in the fridge to splash over a salad – it's also good to use as a quick pickling solution for fruit and vegies.

$^1/_3$ cup extra virgin olive oil
$^1/_3$ cup freshly squeezed lime juice
$^1/_3$ cup rice wine vinegar
1 pinch of salt

Place all ingredients in a bottle and shake to combine.

LIME VINAIGRETTE

Radish and Cucumber Salsa

Char-grilled watermelon Salsa

Pico de Gallo

Roasted Tomato Salsa

Simple Tomato Salsa

ROASTED TOMATO SALSA

Start this recipe 90 minutes before you want to eat it | Makes 2 cups

This is like a roasted Pico de Gallo, and the more you char the tomato skins the tastier it is! It's incredible with pork.

8 whole ripe Roma
   tomatoes, core removed
1 green chili
2 garlic cloves, skins left on
1 white onion, diced
½ cup chopped coriander
   (cilantro)
1 tablespoons freshly
   squeezed lime juice
1 teaspoon salt

Line a frying pan with aluminium foil and place it on the stove on high heat. Place the tomatoes in the pan and dry roast them for five minutes, turning regularly. After five minutes, add green chili and garlic cloves and continue dry roasting for another five minutes until tomatoes, chili and garlic are charred on all sides.

Peel the garlic and place it in a food processor or blender with the tomatoes, green chili, onion and coriander. Process until smooth. Add lime juice and salt to taste. Keeps for 3 days, covered, in the fridge.

SIMPLE TOMATO SALSA

Start this recipe 75 minutes before you want to eat it | Makes 2 cups

Corn chips are my fave food. Topped with a good salsa and they are definitely my fave food. Basic Tomato, Roasted Tomato, and classic Pico de Gallo are great with everything. I've also added a Radish & Cucumber and Watermelon Salsa when you want less heat or more sweet. This salsa is best for piling on top of nachos, fries and hot dogs. Nice and simple.

8 ripe Roma tomatoes, halved, with core removed
1 white onion, peeled
1 teaspoon salt
2 teaspoons sugar
2 tablespoons freshly squeezed lime juice

Dice the tomatoes and onion. Place them in a bowl and add the salt, sugar and lime juice, stirring to combine. Let the salsa sit for at least an hour before serving. Keeps for three days, covered, in the fridge.

Start this recipe 75 minutes before you want to eat it | Makes 2 cups

A classic Mexican salsa, 'pico de gallo' actually means 'rooster's beak' in Spanish. Seriously.

8 ripe Roma tomatoes, halved with the
   core removed
1 white onion, peeled
½ cup finely chopped coriander
   (cilantro)
1 green chili, finely diced
1 teaspoon salt
1 teaspoon sugar
2 tablespoons freshly squeezed lime
   juice

Dice the tomatoes and onion. Place them in a bowl and add the coriander, green chili, salt, sugar and lime juice, stirring to combine. Let the salsa sit for at least an hour before serving. Keeps for 3 days, covered, in the fridge.

PICO DE GALLO

CHAR-GRILLED WATERMELON SALSA

Start this recipe 90 minutes before you want to eat it | Makes 4 cups

The sweetness of the watermelon mixed with the spring onions makes this salsa pretty irresistible. We serve this with corn chips and Jalapeño Cream.

½ a seedless watermelon
½ cup finely chopped
   coriander (cilantro)
½ cup finely chopped
   spring onions
   (eschallots)
2 tablespoons lime juice

Use a knife to cut around the watermelon and remove the rind. Cut the watermelon into 2cm (¾ inch) thick slices. Fire up a char-grill to high heat.

Grill the watermelon for about 2 minutes a side, until charred lines appear. Transfer watermelon to a chopping board and dice into small squares.

In a large bowl, combine the diced watermelon with the coriander, spring onions and lime juice. Stir and let sit for at least an hour before serving. Keeps for 3 days, covered, in the fridge.

RADISH & CUCUMBER SALSA

Start this recipe 2½ hours before you want to eat it | Makes 2 cups

This is really cool salsa, perfect if everything else on your plate is super spicy. It looks great too.

1 bunch of radishes
1 cucumber
1 pickled jalapeño, finely chopped
¼ cup finely chopped coriander (cilantro)
¼ cup finely chopped mint
2 tablespoons freshly squeezed lime juice
1 teaspoon salt

Cut the stems from the radishes and soak them in cool water for half an hour. Scrub the radishes clean and dice them into small cubes, about the size of corn kernels.

Peel the cucumber and dice into cubes of the same size.

Add all the ingredients to a bowl and toss well. Adjust salt and lime juice to taste. Let salsa sit in the fridge for at least two hours before serving.

Start this recipe 5 minutes before you want to eat it | Makes 1 cup

Chipotle is a used a lot in this book. The dense smoky flavour and spice make it one of my favourite ingredients. It's easy to find chipotles in adobo sauce, but you should order a bag of chipotle powder online. It's really cheap for a huge bag and there are at least five recipes in here that use it. I promise you'll get your money's worth!

^{1}/3 cup chipotle powder
^{1}/3 cup sugar
1/3 cup salt

Place ingredients in a small plastic container and shake to combine.

CHIPOTLE SALT

Start this recipe 10 minutes before you want to eat it Serves 4

Sometimes you need more than just salsa on your corn chips.

1 small white onion
1 chipotle in adobo sauce
4 very ripe avocados
juice of one lime
½ cup chopped coriander (cilantro)
salt and pepper

Chop the onion and chipotle very finely. Halve and pit the avocados and scoop the flesh into a large bowl. Mash the avocado with a fork until smooth and cover immediately with the lime juice. Stir through the onion, chipotle and coriander and add salt and pepper to taste.

Allow to sit for 15 minutes before serving.

GUACAMOLE

APPLE & CABBAGE SLAW

Start this recipe 15 minutes before you want to eat it
Serves 6

This sweet and crunchy slaw is great as a side dish and even better on a Pulled Pork sandwich.

½ a green cabbage
5 granny smith apples,
   unpeeled
2 tablespoons lime juice
1 cup whole egg
   mayonnaise
¼ cup rice wine vinegar

Using a coarse grater, grate the cabbage into a bowl. Grate the apples into the bowl, discarding the core. Add the lime juice to the apple so it doesn't go brown. Add the mayonnaise and the vinegar, mixing everything together with your hands.

Start this recipe 15 minutes before you want to eat it Serves 6

Pile some of this slaw up on your plate next to some chicken or beef.

½ **red cabbage**
¼ **cup cider vinegar**
1 **tablespoon olive oil**
2 **tablespoons lime juice**
1 **handful mint leaves**

Cut halved red cabbage into 2 pieces. Using a mandoline, slice the cabbage very finely into a bowl.

Place the vinegar, oil and sugar into a pan and let it simmer over medium heat until the sugar dissolves.

Pour the hot mixture over the cabbage. Add the lime juice and mint leaves and toss until combined. Season with salt to taste. Let the slaw cool in the fridge for half an hour before serving.

RED CABBAGE SLAW

Start this recipe 15 minutes before you want to eat it | Serves 6

Pickles and coleslaw are both terrific things to eat. Why not combine them?

½ green cabbage
8 dill pickles
¼ white onion, finely chopped
½ cup whole egg mayonnaise
¼ cup pickle juice
2 tablespoon lemon juice

Grate the cabbage with a coarse grater. Use a mandoline to julienne the pickles into thin matchsticks. Place cabbage and pickles in a bowl and add onion, mayo, pickle juice and lemon juice. Toss to combine and season with salt and pepper.

DILL PICKLE SLAW

Start this recipe at least a month before you want to eat it | Makes 4 jars

It's good luck to have at least three jars of pickles in your fridge at all times. The best kind of pickles are kosher dill pickles. You can buy a massive jar of them in the kosher section of your supermarket or you can make your own, it's pretty easy. Just buy a ton of cucumbers and spend the afternoon pickling them. A good jar of pickles makes for an incredible gift!

4 x 1 litre (2 pint) jars (you can use different sized jars, as long as combined they can store up to 4 litres), washed thoroughly, rinsed and dried.
2kg (4lbs) pickling cucumbers
2 cups white vinegar

2 litres (4 pints) of water
100g (3½ oz) coarse salt
2 bunches of dill, roughly chopped
4 cloves of garlic, peeled and halved
2 teaspoons mustard seeds
2 teaspoons black peppercorns

Wash the cucumbers thoroughly and leave them to soak in ice cold water for two hours.

Sterilize your jars. Find the biggest pan you own (it needs to be big enough to fully submerge a jar inside) and fill it with water. Bring it to the boil and submerge each jar and lid inside for 10 minutes.

While the jars are sterilizing, place another pan on the stove and bring the vinegar, water and salt to the boil. This is your brine.

Remove the cucumbers from their bath and take off a really thin slice from each end with your knife.

In each jar, place a handful of chopped dill, 2 half cloves of garlic and a teaspoon each of the mustard seeds and peppercorns. Place enough cucumbers inside to fill the jar, then sprinkle a little more dill over the top before filling each jar with the hot brine. Seal the jars tightly, making sure you've cleaned any residue from the rim.

Submerge each jar back into the big pan of boiling water for another five minutes to seal the jars one more time. Once removed, teach yourself how to play the accordion during the 4–6 weeks it takes for the pickles to be ready. Refrigerate jars after opening.

DILL PICKLES

GRANNY ANNIE'S POTATO SALAD

Start this recipe at least 3 hours before you want to eat it | Serves 6

Food has always been a big focus at my family's get-togethers. Sure we love each other, but we also love eating, especially with each other. In my decades of birthday dinners and Christmas lunches, my family has gone through their fair share of food trends, but my grandma's potato salad has been on the menu every time. Probably because it's the greatest potato salad in the universe and Granny Annie is a hero for giving it to me.

2kg (4lb) Desiree potatoes, washed
6 tablespoons whole egg mayonnaise
4 tablespoons sour cream
2 tablespoon cream
½ bunch of mint, finely chopped
½ bunch of parsley, finely chopped
1 brown onion, finely diced
4 eggs, hard-boiled
salt and pepper

Place the potatoes in a pan of cool water and add a tablespoon of salt. Bring to the boil over high heat. Leave the pan to boil for 25 minutes, until the potatoes are tender. Drain the potatoes and leave to cool.

When the potatoes are cool enough to touch, peel the skins off and cut the potatoes into medium-sized cubes. Leave them aside in a large bowl.

In another bowl, combine the mayonnaise with the creams. Add the chopped herbs.

Slice the hard-boiled eggs into quarters and cut each quarter into four pieces. Scatter the eggs and onion over the potatoes. Pour the mayonnaise mixture over the potatoes and toss to combine everything. Add salt and black pepper to taste.

Chill in the fridge for a couple of hours and serve cold. With every bite, feel guilty that you haven't called your Granny in a long while.

Start this recipe 30 minutes before you want to eat it | Serves 6

This is a fun way to cook vegies on your barbecue. Feel free to add the greens of your choice to the foil packets. Snow peas, asparagus and green capsicum work nicely. Mix it up!

500g (1lb) sugar snap peas [mange tout]
500g (1lb) brussels sprouts
1kg (2lb) broccoli
¼ cup finely chopped coriander (cilantro)
½ cup Lime Vinaigrette (see Sauces, Salsas, Salads & Sides)
1 tablespoon Chipotle Salt (see Sauces, Salsas, Salads & Sides)

Wash all the vegies and cut the tops and tails off the sugar snap peas. Slice the ends off the brussels sprouts and cut them in half. Cut the broccoli into medium-sized florets, discarding the stalks. Mix all the vegies together in a big bowl.

Lay two pieces of aluminium foil, about 30 x 50cm (12 x 20 ins), flat on bench. Place 2 cups of the vegetables in the centre of the foil. Fold up the ends and seal the greens in a little parcel. Make sure the foil doesn't double up; you only want one thickness all the way around.

Place the foil parcels on a hot barbecue grill or char-grill pan and cook for four minutes a side. Take the parcels off the grill and wearing oven mitts, open the foil parcels carefully, allowing the steam to escape. Empty the vegetables into a bowl and toss through the vinaigrette and coriander. Sprinkle the chipotle salt over the top and serve.

In each jar, place a handful of chopped dill, 2 half cloves of

GRILLED GREENS

Start this recipe 30 minutes before you want to eat it | Serves 4

Grilled corn is the ultimate side dish at a barbecue. The sweet, crunchy kernels are a great way to balance out a meal mostly of meat.

4 cobs of corn, shucked
1 cup Lime mayo (see Sauces, Salsas, Salads & Sides)
2 tablespoons Chipotle salt (see Sauces, Salsas, Salads & Sides)
2 tablespoons finely chopped coriander (cilantro)

Place the corn in a pan of boiling water and cook for 5 minutes until each cob is a vibrant yellow. Remove the corn from the water and take it straight to the barbecue, grilling each cob for 6 minutes, turning repeatedly until charred (but not burnt) all over.

Serve the grilled corn slathered in Lime mayo, with Chipotle salt and coriander sprinkled over the top.

GRILLED CORN

Start this recipe 90 minutes before you want to eat it | Serves 4

Putting the extra effort into making macaroni and cheese from scratch will leave you feeling a lot better about yourself than the 'I'm a silly, chubby kid' feeling you get after eating a bowl of the boxed supermarket mac & cheese. In the fairly unlikely event that you have any leftover, you should try making some Grilled Mac & Cheese sandwiches the next day (see Burgers, Sandwiches & Hot Dogs)

2 cups macaroni
3 tablespoons salted butter
1 tablespoon plain flour
2 cups milk
1 cup cream
3 cups sharp cheddar cheese, finely
    grated
2 tablespoons parmesan, finely grated
1 teaspoon ground white pepper
1 teaspoon sweet paprika

Cook the macaroni in a pan of salted boiling water until 'al dente'. Drain and place noodles aside.

Heat oven to 180°C/350°F. In a saucepan, melt the butter over medium heat. Add the flour to the pan and whisk for two minutes. Slowly add the milk and cream, whisking constantly. When it starts to simmer, reduce the heat to low and add 2 cups of the cheddar cheese and all of the parmesan. Add the white pepper and season with salt. Remove from heat.

Add the cooked noodles to the pan and stir until combined. Pour the mixture into a baking dish and sprinkle the remaining cheddar over the top. Using your fingers, sprinkle the paprika evenly over the top of the cheese.

Bake in the oven for 40 minutes, until the top of the cheese has browned. Allow to cool for 10 minutes and serve.

This tastes amazing with some Dynamite Beef Chili (see Slow Cooked Stuff) on the side!

MAC & CHEESE

SWEET
STUFF

Makes 8 serves

This is a dessert version of the standard corn chips, guacamole and salsa. Instead of starting the meal with it, end your meal with this sweet version

AVOCADO ICE CREAM

4 ripe avocados, skin and stone removed
2 cups sour cream
1 cup thickened cream
1½ cups sugar
2 tablespoons freshly squeezed lime juice
2 pinches salt

Makes 1 litre (2 pints)
Place all the ingredients into a food processor and blend until smooth. It should be an awesome shade of green.

Refrigerate the mixture for at least 6 hours. Transfer mixture to an ice cream maker and freeze according to manufacturer's instructions.

STRAWBERRY SALSA

1 punnet of strawberries, washed and hulled
1 tablespoon finely chopped mint
1 tablespoon sugar
1 tablespoon freshly squeezed lime juice
1 teaspoon vanilla essence
4 waffle ice cream cones, broken into big pieces

Makes 1 cup
To make strawberry salsa, chop the strawberries into small cubes and transfer them to a bowl. Add the mint, sugar, lime juice and vanilla essence and stir until well combined. Refrigerate for an hour before using.

Get a nice big scoop of the avocado ice cream and put it in a bowl. Spoon some of the strawberry salsa next to the avocado ice cream. Place two pieces of the waffle cone into the ice cream and serve.

ICE COLD GUAC

Start making this 1 day before you want to eat it | Makes 40 ice cream sandwiches

This awesome ice cream sandwich was super popular at The Dip, but half the diners would spend too long trying to get the perfect photo of it and the ice cream would melt! The cookie is soft and chewy and the caramel ice cream beautifully rich, topped with a wicked hot fudge. Try eating this with your hands but you'll have better luck eating it with a spoon.

CHOCOLATE MOLASSES COOKIES

375g (13oz) dark chocolate chips
340g (12oz) butter, cut into small cubes
2 cups brown sugar
3 eggs, lightly beaten
3 teaspoon vanilla
½ cup molasses
4½ cups flour
¾ teaspoon salt

Bring a pan of water to a simmer and place a metallic bowl big enough to the cover the pan over the water. Put the chocolate and butter in the bowl and stir until the mixture has melted completely. Alternatively you can do this in the microwave, just put the chocolate and butter in a microwave safe bowl and microwave in 30 second increments, stirring in between, until the mixture has completely melted.

Combine the brown sugar, eggs, vanilla and molasses in a bowl and stir until smooth.

Combine the flour and salt in a bowl and add the brown sugar mixture and the melted chocolate. Stir until smooth and well combined. Cover the bowl with cling film and chill mixture in the refrigerator for an hour.

Heat the oven to 180°C/350°F. Line a baking tray with baking paper and remove the mixture from the fridge.

Use a teaspoon to make a small ball of the mixture and roll it with your hands. Press each ball onto the baking paper, leaving 2½cms (1ins) in between each ball. Bake for 10 minutes, remove from oven and let the cookies cool.

COOKIES & CREAM

SALTED CARAMEL ICE CREAM

Makes 1 litre (2 pints)

1½ cups white sugar
60g (2oz) butter, cut into small
  cubes
1 teaspoon salt
2 cups thickened cream
2 cups cold milk
4 egg yolks

Heat the sugar in a pan over medium heat until the sugar at the edge of the pan starts to melt. Using a wooden spoon, slowly stir the sugar towards the middle of the pan. Keep heating until the sugar has completely melted and starts to brown. Once the sugar has reached a nice amber colour, add the salt and remove from the heat.

Add the butter and stir until it's melted into the sugar. Place the pan back onto the heat and slowly add the cream, stirring well to make caramel. Remove from the heat.

Whisk the egg yolks in a bowl and slowly add half a cup of the hot caramel, stirring the eggs as you pour. Add the warmed yolks to the pan and place back over medium heat.

Stir the mixture until it thickens, making sure it doesn't stick to the bottom of the pan.

Pour the milk into a large bowl and add the caramel mixture. Stir until well combined. Refrigerate for 6 hours and transfer it to an ice cream maker. Freeze according to the manufacturer's instructions.

This recipe was texted to me an hour before The Dip first opened by my friend Dan Hong. Thanks Hongy!

HOT CHOCOLATE FUDGE

160ml (5½ fl oz) water
140g (5oz) glucose
1 tablespoon cocoa
20g (¾ oz) butter
130g (4½oz) dark chocolate,
    broken into small pieces
½ teaspoon salt

Pour the water, glucose and cocoa into a pan and bring to the boil over medium heat.

Add the butter and chocolate and stir until melted and well combined. Bring back to the boil and remove from heat. Season with salt to taste.

Fill a small squeezy sauce bottle with the chocolate fudge sauce. Place one cookie in a bowl and scoop a big scoop of the salted caramel ice cream on top. Place another cookie on top of the ice cream and add a cross of fudge sauce over the top. Yum.

This epic looking dessert is actually pretty easy to make - you can use any chocolate coated cookies, or even chocolate bars like Kit Kats, Mars Bars and even Maltesers. Chuck 'em all in there. Party time.

CHOC COOKIE TERRINE

5 cups (about 900g/2lbs) good quality milk chocolate
2 cups thickened cream
2 packets of your favorite chocolate coated cookies

First we need to make a chocolate ganache. Crumble the chocolate into a heatproof bowl and pour the cream into a pot. Bring the pot of cream to a boil and pour it over the chocolate, stirring well until all the chocolate is completely melted.

Get out your terrine mold. You can use a loaf pan if you don't have a proper mold, you will need to line it with cling film though.

Pour some of the ganache into the bottom of the mould, then add a layer of chocolate cookies, pushed snugly next to each other. Pour some ganache over the cookies, then add another layer of cookies. Continue this until you have run out of cookies! Finish the terrine with the last of the ganache. Use a knife to make sure the top of the terrine is smooth.

Transfer the terrine to a fridge and let it set for at least 3 hours. Once set, cut the terrine into thick slices to serve. It tastes great with strawberry milkshake ice cream.

PEANUT BUTTER JELLY SANDWICH

Start this recipe 6 hours before you want to eat it | Serves 6

Kids on *Sesame Street* always used to eat peanut butter and jelly sandwiches and it used to blow my little mind. It seriously sounded like the most disgusting thing ever. When I eventually tried one I loved it, but always thought it would be better as dessert instead of lunch.

PEANUT BUTTER ICE CREAM

1 cup smooth peanut butter
2 cups thickened cream
2 cups sour cream
½ cup sugar
1 teaspoon vanilla

Makes 1 litre (2 pints)
Spoon all ingredients into a food processor and blend until smooth. Chill the mixture in the fridge for at least 4 hours. Transfer the mixture to an ice cream maker and freeze according to manufacturer's instructions.

SPICY PEANUT BRITTLE

2½ cups sugar
½ cup peanuts
1 teaspoon chipotle powder
1 teaspoon cinnamon
50g (1½ oz) butter, cut into small
  cubes

Place the sugar in a pan, add ½ cup of water and stir. Bring the water to the boil over medium heat. Once it starts to boil, cover the pan and allow it to boil for 2 minutes. Remove the lid and let the sugar boil for another 20 minutes until it turns golden.

While the sugar is boiling, line a baking tray with baking paper and set aside. Combine the peanuts, chipotle powder and cinnamon in a bowl and mix well.

Once the sugar has turned a nice golden colour, remove it from the heat and stir the butter through with a wooden spoon. Stir through the nuts and spices and pour the mixture over the baking tray lined with baking paper. Tilt the tray backwards and forwards to spread the sugar, creating as thin a layer of toffee as possible.

Set the toffee aside to cool and harden. Once it has hardened, break it into pieces and store it in a plastic container until ready to use.

250g (½lb) raspberry jam
25g (¾oz) butter, cut into small cubes
1 teaspoon freshly squeezed lime juice

For the sandwiches:
6 mini brioche rolls cut in half, or larger brioche rolls cut into small pieces

Spoon jam into a pan with ¼ cup of water and butter. Bring to a simmer over low heat and let it bubble for 20 minutes, until it has thickened. Remove from the heat and add the lime juice to taste. Transfer the raspberry mixture to a small plastic squeeze bottle and allow to cool in the fridge for an hour.

SANDWICH ASSEMBLY

Toast the brioche on each side and arrange the two halves side by side in a bowl. Place a big scoop of peanut butter ice cream in between to the two pieces of brioche.

Squirt a zig zag of raspberry jelly over the brioche and ice cream and stick a big shard of peanut brittle into the ice cream.

RASPBERRY JELLY

Makes 1 litre (2 pints) Start this recipe at least 6 hours before you want to eat it | Makes a little less than a litre (2 pints)

This is the ultimate cheat's ice cream! When I was in high school me and my friends used to get drunk on milkshakes from the corner store near the station. You could find us seated around a metal table, our uniforms untucked, with a handful of potato wedges in one hand and a milkshake in the other.

My fave milkshake flavor was always lime. It didn't taste anything like lime, but it was a beautiful shade of green. I always wanted to make it into an ice cream and I finally figured out a way to get that creamy milkshake consistency. We've made pineapple, banana, chocolate and strawberry ice cream using this recipe and they've all been crazy good. The sour cream freezes so well, with such great creaminess that this is a good recipe to try out even if you don't have an ice cream machine – just pour the mixture into a container and pop it in the freezer, stirring every half hour until it freezes!

1 cup milkshake topping or ice
  cream syrup
1 cup thickened cream
2 cups sour cream

Pour all ingredients into a food processor and blend until smooth. Pour the mixture into an ice cream maker and freeze according to manufacturer's instructions.

Serve with fruit, chocolate or anything that makes you feel nostalgic.

MILKSHAKE ICE CREAM

GRILLED PINEAPPLE & COCONUT ICE CREAM

Start this recipe at least 8 hours before you wanna eat it | Serves 8

What's better than taking a nice healthy piece of fruit, dunking it in booze and butter, grilling it and serving it with ice cream? We called this dessert the 'Yo Ho Ho' when it was on our menu. Pirates love it.

½ cup dark rum
½ cup brown sugar
2 tablespoons butter
1 pineapple, peeled and cored, sliced into wedges lengthwise
2 tablespoons shredded coconut

Coconut Ice Cream:
1 cup coconut milk
1 cup sour cream
1 cup thickened cream
½ cup white sugar
1 teaspoon vanilla essence

To make coconut ice cream, combine the coconut milk, sour cream, thickened cream, white sugar and vanilla in a food processor and blend until smooth. Let chill in the fridge for at least 4 hours. Add mixture to an ice cream maker and freeze according to manufacturer's instructions. Place the rum, brown sugar and butter together in a pan and bring to a simmer over a low heat, simmer for 20 minutes and remove from heat. Place the pieces of pineapple in the rum mixture and allow them to soak for an hour. Preheat the oven for 180°C/350°F. Scatter the coconut across a baking tray and bake for 3 minutes, then remove the tray and mix the coconut around before putting it back in the oven for another 3 minutes. Repeat this process until the coconut is brown and toasted, being careful not to burn it! Preheat a barbecue grill plate or char-grill pan to high heat. Grill the pieces of pineapple for 3 minutes each side until it starts to caramelize. Place a piece of pineapple in each bowl and spoon some of the leftover rum caramel over the top. Place a big scoop of the coconut ice cream next to the pineapple and scatter some toasted coconut over the top. Serve.

Start this recipe 2 hours before you want to eat it | Serves 6

When I first told people I was selling this, people assumed I was pouring a can of cola into the deep fryer, scooping oily sugar into a bowl and laughing at whoever bought one. These are more like cola-flavoured donuts, hot out of the fryer and covered in syrup, dusted in cinnamon sugar, topped with whipped cream and, of course, a cherry on top. If you prefer a cherry cola, buy some cherry bitters and add a few drops to the cola syrup.

2 cups plain flour
1 teaspoon baking powder
2 eggs, beaten
1½ cups, plus 6 tablespoons
   extra, cola syrup or cola
   flavoured cordial
1 cup cream
2 tablespoons icing sugar
½ teaspoon vanilla
2 teaspoons cinnamon

Combine flour and baking powder in a bowl. Add the eggs and cola syrup to the flour and whisk until combined. Freeze for one hour.

Put cream in a bowl and stir in half the icing sugar and vanilla. Whip the cream with electric beaters until thick and fluffy.

Mix together the remaining icing sugar and the cinnamon in a bowl.

Heat oil in a deep fryer or frying pan to 180°C/350°F. Use a spoon to scoop out little balls of the batter and drop them into the oil. Leave each ball to cook for about 90 seconds, until they float to the top and start to brown.

To serve, put 6 of the deep fried cola balls into a cup and pour a tablespoon of cola syrup over the top. Sprinkle the cinnamon icing sugar over the cola balls and add a dollop of the whipped cream. Place a cherry on top of the cream and serve with a spoon and straw.

DEEP FRIED COLA SUNDAE

Start this recipe 3 hours before you want to eat it | Makes 24 cupcakes

At every birthday celebration in my family, no matter how old the person is, there are always cupcakes. This recipe comes from my mum's cookbook, who copied it out of her grandmother's cookbook decades ago, and my sisters still use it today. So naturally I'm gonna ruin everything and suggest everybody deep fry this proud family tradition.

24 cupcake patty cases
125g (4½oz) butter, at room temperature
2 eggs, at room temperature
¾ cup sugar
1½ cups self-raising flour
½ cup milk
1 teaspoon vanilla essence
24 popsicle sticks or wooden chopsticks

Chocolate Icing:
50g (1½ oz) butter, at room temperature
1 cup icing sugar
food colouring
1 tablespoon milk (optional)
sprinkles

Batter:
2 eggs
1⅓ cup milk
3 tablespoon sugar
2½ cups flour
½ teaspoon salt
2 teaspoons baking soda

To make the cupcakes, line a 24 hole cupcake tray with patty cases.

Mix the butter, eggs, sugar, flour, milk and vanilla together in a bowl until smooth and fluffy. Use an electric mixer if you have one, or work on your biceps and do it by hand.

Preheat oven to 210°C/410°F. Spoon mixture evenly into patty cases and bake for 10–15 minutes until browned on top. Push a skewer through a cupcake and if it comes out clean, the cakes are cooked. Let cupcakes cool. To make the icing, cream the butter in a bowl with an electric mixer until fluffy. Add the icing sugar and a few drops of food colouring, stirring it through the butter with a wooden spoon until smooth. You may need to add a little milk to thin the icing out. Spread a thin layer of icing over each cake and top with sprinkles. Leave icing to set on cakes for 30 minutes.

To make the batter, beat the eggs into the milk in a bowl. Stir in the sugar, flour, salt and baking powder and whisk until smooth and thick. Heat cooking oil in a deep fryer or saucepan to 180°C/250°F. Remove the paper cases from the cupcakes and stick a paddle pop stick into the bottom of each of them. Put on a pair of thick rubber gloves for safety. Holding the paddle pop stick, dip each cupcake in the batter, rolling each one around to ensure it gets a nice all over coating. Quickly dip each cupcake into the deep fryer, for about 90 seconds until the batter turns golden.

DEEP FRIED CAKES

DEEP-FRIED BANANA SPLIT

Make a healthy banana even healthier by giving it a day spa in burning hot oil and then covering it in relaxing ice cream and chocolate. Good for the mind, body and soul.

PEANUT BUTTER ICE CREAM

Makes 1 litre (2 pints)

1 cup smooth peanut butter
2 cups thickened cream
2 cups sour cream
½ cup sugar
1 teaspoon vanilla

Spoon all ingredients into a food processor and blend until smooth. Chill the mixture in the fridge for at least 4 hours.

Transfer the mixture to an ice cream maker and freeze overnight according to manufacturer's instructions.

HOT CHOCOLATE FUDGE

160ml (5½ fl oz) water
140g (5oz) glucose
1 tablespoon cocoa
20g (¾ oz) butter
130g (4½oz) dark chocolate,
   broken into small pieces
½ teaspoon salt

Pour the water, glucose and cocoa into a pan and bring to the boil over medium heat.

Add the butter and chocolate and stir until melted and well combined. Bring back to the boil and remove from heat. Season with salt to taste and transfer to a plastic squeezy bottle.

Banana:
4 ripe bananas
¼ cup plain flour
1 tsp cinnamon
¼ cup crushed salted peanuts

BANANA SPLIT ASSEMBLY

To assemble the banana split, peel the bananas and slice them lengthways. Combine the cinnamon and flour in a bowl and roll the banana halves in the flour unti they are coated.

Set your deep fryer to 180°C/250°F and add each banana half, two pieces at a time. Allow them to cook for 2 minutes until golden. Remove the bananas from the oil and transfer them onto paper towels to absorb any excess oil.

Place two halves of a banana in a bowl and top with a scoop of peanut butter ice cream. Add a squiggle of hot chocolate fudge and scatter some peanuts over the top. Serve.

INDEX

Published in 2014 by
New Holland Publishers Pty Ltd   FEB 0 2 2016
London • Sydney • Auckland

The Chandlery Unit 009 50 Westminster Bridge Road London SE1 7QY United Kingdom
1/66 Gibbes Street Chatswood NSW 2067 Australia
218 Lake Road Northcote Auckland New Zealand

www.newhollandpublishers.com

Copyright © 2014 New Holland Publishers
Copyright © 2014 in text: Andrew Levins
Copyright © 2014 in images: NHIL
Except iStockphotos on pages 8, 51, 86-87, 106, 109, 128, 171
Photo credits to Thomas Walk for pages 32, 60-61, 62, 104-105, 124, 146-147

A record of this book is held at the British Library and the National Library of Australia

ISBN   9781742576404

Publisher: Fiona Schultz
Designer: Andrew Quinlan
Food stylist: Jodi Wuestewald, with thanks to Mud Australia and Market Imports
Production director: Olga Dementiev
Printer: Toppan Leefung (China) Ltd

10 9 8 7 6 5 4 3 2 1

Keep up with New Holland Publishers on Facebook http://www.facebook.com/NewHollandPublishers